cally just a big dump—that's were the dump is, as well as all the recycling centers . . . two-day-old burrito: though soggy, good . . . crossing the Willamette River at 26 mph into Springfield (makes me think of a bad NOFX song) . . . a pint of Lagunitas Lucky 13, the only beer I have . . . screeching . . . into Springfield's yard at 26 mph, passing a half-shuttered industry to the left and, looking out overtop tankers, the Roseboro lumber yard to the right . . . the mainline passes right through the middle of Springfield's yard so you're always in the middle of trains . . . *32 mph coming out the end of Springfield's yard past the lumber company's loading area—make that 37 mph . . . barreling through the dark, starry farmlands of Pleasant Hill at 46 mph . . . Kesey country . . .*

Eugene yard sunset from the DPU

*

It's the middle of the night and I'm at Frazier. There's no mistaking it, this is Frazier: there are no trees on the hill but there's a brand new barricade and a wire fence to protect from falling boulders; on the other side it's a straight drop off and you can hear all the way across the valley (I actually hear a train passing at the lower spot where the tracks loop below).

I've been hiding for about an hour from two very vigilant workers with spotlight-strength flashlights—very bright—who roamed the train down one side and then came back up on both looking for me, and it's the middle of the night. There was an older worker and a younger worker, and I heard Older Worker telling Younger Worker how looking for train-riders was like hunting. He told Younger Worker that Younger Worker'd be surprised how Older Worker's climbed up and found kids hiding on top of train cars. Younger Worker then scaled the ladder on a hopper right across from where I was hiding and yelled, *You up there?* But I wasn't. Older Worker then told Younger Worker not to worry too much because I wasn't a serial killer or anything, just another traveler.

The rear unit (DPU) is now locked. I walked all the way back to it but wasn't able to get on, and luckily I had time to get back up to another rideable before the train took off. Now I'm on the back porch of a UP hopper with not much of a cubbyhole, the train is again moving, and I'm dreading going into K-Falls...

*

The train has stopped again at the next siding and I'm again hiding in the mountains. I heard a train down below at Frazier, so that train is likely to pass soon. It would be nice if I could catch-on to that train somehow, like if it for some reason stopped on the mainline and I could switch to it. Or maybe this train will stop on a siding before K-Falls, at say Chiloquin or Modoc Point, and I can abandon it, sleep some time away, and then hitchhike the rest of the way to K-Falls. Otherwise, I'm in for a rough arrival when I get there. (I'd do about anything to not get a court date riding this train). It's foggy out over the Cascades—very foggy—and I can hear streams trickling from far away. Around the bend I can almost hear the front units idling ahead, but it's too dark to see much besides the silhouette of the train against the sky and the sky reflecting off the rails some. I'm going to cross over to the dark side of the train and walk back to see if any of the boxcars are perhaps open on the other side, but I don't think they are. I'm pretty sure there's a train coming up from behind that's going to pass me here. It's about 2 a.m.

Klamath Falls, OR- It's already hot here and I've never seen so many bugs in all my life. All around are gnats and tiny insects festering on the surface of the water, in the shade, in the dirt, and basically just forming huge fluttering clouds that I keep having to walk through. I climbed off the train onto the mainline this morning and stood looking down on some high school sports field on one side and a small channel on the other. I walked right onto Esplanade St. and found the Green Blade Bakery, which looks more like a check-cashing service than a bakery by the looks of the building that it's in, and must be a Christian establishment or something because the people are all so god-awful nice. But what a welcome change it is from last night...

After waiting ten hours for a train, I finally caught south out of Eugene in a DPU and rode it up into the Cascades. Somewheres well past Oakridge, while climbing the backside of Coyote Mountain on a hairpin curve on the Cascade Loops, I awoke to a beer-full bladder and stepped out onto the catwalk to micturate. When I came back in I was caught a little off balance by the rocking of the unit and, with my shoulder, fell into the back wall next to the door, slamming into an area of panels with buttons that always have a plastic-like display case protecting them, but on this decrepit engine didn't, and my shoulder hit a big round red plug of a button and effectively killed the rear unit instantly. It was obvious as shit when it happened too as everything went silent, and I could soon feel the rear unit lunging as it was literally being dragged up the slope. Within a minute a bell in the cab went off like a rotary-telephone ringing non-stop and I watched the speedometer slowly decline from 14 to 13 to 12 as I stuffed my belongings into my pack. The train stopped dead on the mainline about a mile later and I climbed off into the darkness. This was at Frazier, I soon discerned, because the whole mountainside was landslide-wiped-out and newly reinforced. I walked in the pitch-black between the train and a wire boulder-catching fence, at the base of which was a low wall of concrete traffic barricades buttressing the hillside. When I saw flashlights approaching, that's where I hid, behind the barricade, lying on my stomach on the rocks and weeds with who-knows-what. I had my bag stashed in

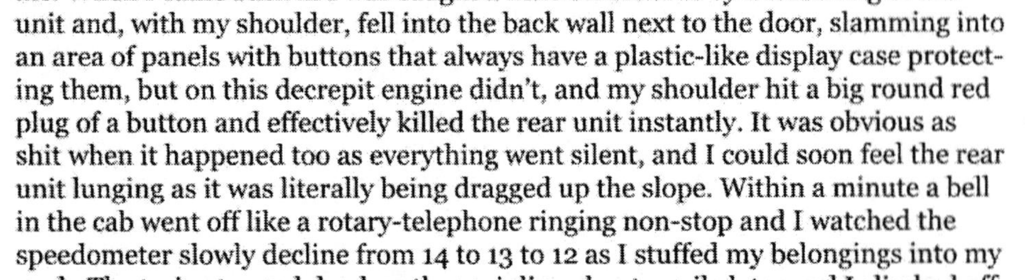

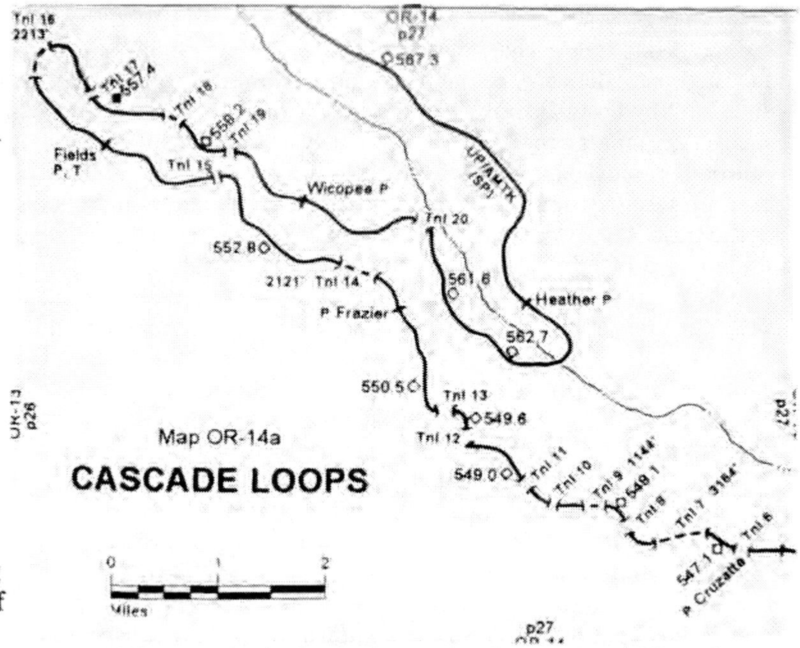

the cubby-hole of a big-belly Canadian grainer, which wasn't very smart (having it separate from me), because by the time I saw the workers' flashlights approaching I wasn't able to get my bag out for fear of drawing too much attention to myself in the utterly dead silence. So I left my bag hiding there on the train while I hid myself behind the barricades adjacent. But the workers were on to me. They must've known from the moment the engine died that it was due to *human* error and nothing malfunctional; they were looking for train-riders, and they scoured every porch until they found one.

"Good evening Fellas," the Engineer said to my bag. (I take it this was the Engineer because he was obviously more confident and experienced (as well as older), and I remember thinking back in Eugene how experienced and skilled the Engineer of the train must be in order to move it from a dead standstill without any clanking or slacking of the couplers). I stayed hidden in the shadows behind the concrete but I could hear him talking clearly and I could see the shadows from their flashlights exploring the area around the porch.

The Engineer informed my bag, speaking to it as if it were a guilty couple of crusty train-hoppers (obviously talking loud enough that whoever was hiding nearby could hear), that when the train reached Klamath Falls it would be subject to extensive search by the Police, and so it was best to not be on the train when it arrived (considerate of him really). On a notepad he wrote down the car initials and serial number, then he and the younger worker proceeded back the rest of the train to restart the DPU. I was surprised he did not confiscate my bag on the spot, or at least unload it off the train. I mean, I don't know what I would've done if he had, other than come out of hiding to claim it, but for whatever bizarre reason he left it alone.

As soon as they were gone I rescued my admonished bag from the porch and walked the line up the opposite way. I then hid *with* my bag back behind the concrete barricade, but in a different place entirely. The unit in the rear rumbled back to life in the fog and soon the workers came walking back up, one on each side of the train. After seeing that my bag was now *gone*, they began searching more thoroughly, creatively, but still not looking behind the barricade where I was hiding. When they arrived next to where I was lying on my stomach in the weeds, the Engineer (the older of the two) was explaining to the younger guy his experience looking for train-hoppers, and how it was like hunting, mentally, like a game with a very smart prey. (He was obviously a very weathered and knowledgeable railroad employee familiar with train-hopper habits and tendencies, especially their preference to ride DPUs). Minutes before, I had thought about hiding on top of the train, but decided against it because I would essentially be cornering myself; and I'm glad I didn't because the older worker told the younger worker how he'd found three kids hiding atop a hopper before; and at his direction, the Younger Worker climbed the ladder to the top of a hopper and hollered into the headlamp-illuminated fog, Are you up there? When they realized I was not and couldn't find me, the Older Worker imparted to the Younger Worker (quite wisely, I'd say): "Well, it doesn't really matter anyway. This is just another traveler; it's not Ramirez or anything."

I remember him saying that clear as day. He was referring to serial killer Angel Resendez, commonly known in the media as Rafael Resendez-Ramirez, one of a multitude of his aliases the FBI latched onto before they were able to positively ID him. (Rafael Resendez-Ramirez was actually the name of one of his uncles, but he also adopted Ramirez as a sort of ode to late-80s serial killer Richard Ramirez, AKA "The Night Stalker," who was known to carve satanic symbols into the bodies of his victims, a practice that Resendez-Ramirez also later copied). Resendez-Ramirez was a Mexican immigrant who earned the nickname "The Railroad Killer" based on the fact that many of his victims were found in their marauded homes near railroad tracks. He himself often hopped freight trains to get around the country and across the border and back. Responsible for at least thirteen murders in states such as Florida, Texas, Kentucky, Georgia, and Illinois, Resendez-Ramirez' actions initiated a nation-wide manhunt called Operation Stop Train that terrified the public for many months and, as a result, projected a negative stereotype on both hobos and young Mexican men that lasted well beyond his surrender to Texas Rangers in El Paso, July 1999. Paranoia and lore followed his rampage, permeating society and the railroad industry to the extent that to this day the first thing people often associate with hopping trains is that a lot of perennially dangerous, crazed killers do it. Law enforcement in turn has perpetuated that stereotype as a means to discourage trespassing on federal property, and to this day the image remains prevalent. (I myself have had the stereotype thrown at me multiple times throughout the past decade by various arms of the law all across the country. But in support of the crazed-psycho-hobo-mafia stereotype, Ramirez wasn't the only freight-train-riding serial killer in the 90s. There was also Robert Silveria, AKA Sidetrack, of FTRA infamy, who confessed to upwards of thirty separate murders, including at least two in the state of Oregon (one occurring on a train ride that originated in Eugene, and the other in Salem's train yard). The Sidetrack case was eventually cracked by a Salem Oregon detective with the help of a rare witness providing one tiny bit of visual evidence: a tattoo on Silveria's neck above the shirtline that read "Freedom"). But at least this engineer was a little better educated and not entirely brainwashed by media hysteria.

After the workers left I immediately went to look for another car to ride, then thought, *Why not just get back on the DPU?* But the DPU was now locked—at *both* doors. So halfway back up the line I settled on the back porch of a UP

SALEM POLICE DEPARTMENT INFORMATION BULLETIN HOMICIDE VICTIM/SUSPECT

On December 1, 1995 William Avis PETTIT, Jr. was murdered in Salem, Oregon. His body was found inside a railroad boxcar. Pettit had been a long time train rider. Investigation of PETTIT'S murder has revealed a suspect. In March of 1996 a Robert Joseph SILVERA was arrested for the murder of PETTIT. SILVERA is also a suspect in numerous other homicides of transients across the United States. SILVERA is also a long time train rider and goes by the name **"SIDETRACK"**.

Any person who knows SILVERA, AKA "Sidetrack" or the victim PETTIT is asked to contact Salem Police Department at 503-588-6050. Please ask for Detective Mike Quakenbush. All calls can be made collect, and the callers can remain anonymous.

SILVERIA
ROBERT JOSEPH
DOB: 03/03/59
RACE: WHITE
SEX: MALE
HEIGHT: 6'01
WEIGHT: 180
EYE COLOR: BLUE
HAIR COLOR: BROWN
PHOTO DATE: 03/14/96
PHOTO NUM: 705826

hopper, one with only a small cubbyhole that my bag would hardly fit in. When the train finally aired up and moved on, I didn't even bother getting my sleeping bag out. The train rolled on only as far as the next siding, then stopped. Thinking the worst was over, I laid there on my sleeping mat and could hear a train off in the distance somewhere on the tracks below, but I was deep in the High Cascades, it was the middle of the night, and I fell lightly asleep. But the sound of gravel crunching soon woke me. I sat up and looked down the cliff and saw the headlights of two or three vehicles climbing up the dark forest-service road, and I knew it could only mean one thing.

In no time, more spotlights came at me from the back end of the train, and knowing it was not just workers this time, I scampered down the cliffside to hide. However, I became trapped as the unstable cliff began to give way, sending rocks cascading loudly down the ravine. I hung there perilously as two Sheriffs with basically searchlights approached—one on each side of the train and about five car lengths apart. I tried to somehow cross the slope and find stable footing because the cliff was not holding and rocks continued to dislodge and create the only noise other than the Sheriff's feet. But passing trains somehow always seem to come at the most miraculous times. Here came that southbound I had heard below, adding brightly to the searchlights, making it like daylight in the dead of night. The miracle was that the monstrous, slow-moving hotshot drowned out any and all noise that I made, or would make, allowing me some direly needed breathing room—an enormous bubble of air in a deep, dark ocean depth. I found stable footing on some large rocks and old railroad ties embedded in the cliffside, and continued to cling there motionlessly. The Sheriff, meanwhile, either being brave or foolish—I don't know—stayed next to the sided train he was searching so that he was walking in between the two lines when the passing hotshot came. And even more fortunate for me was that all of this chaos happened just as the Sheriff was passing directly above where I was straddling the cliff. I peaked nervously up at his flashlight systematically scanning each train that passed, occasionally flickering over to the cliffside and illuminating the forest to my left, and I remained there until the hotshot had passed entirely and both Sheriffs were long gone. Only then did I climb carefully back up the slope and hightail it back to the other end of the train. And then, stupid or not, I went right back to the big-belly grainer where my bag had been stashed and spotted earlier. Its cubbyholes—two spacious ones on each side—provided the best option for a place to hide, and since they had already in-

uh-oh

spected the train a couple of times, I thought I would be safe there.

I could see the DPU glowing through the fog next to the headlights of multiple law enforcement vehicles as I climbed back onto the hopper. I hid my bags far back in the cubbyhole, up against the front so that if you were looking in from the tracks you could not see them, and I waited to hide myself until flashlights reappeared up the tracks. When I saw the Sheriffs returning on the mainline, I climbed in and sat silently on the mainline-side, my back as close to the front of the cubbyhole as I could squeeze myself, and my feet as far out of the way as contortionly possible. But the two Sheriffs, now with the Engineer, walked right up to the cubbyhole I was stowed away in and shined their lights inside.

"This is where they *used* to be," the Engineer said. He then explained that the cubbyholes were actually quite roomy. "Go ahead, you can stick your head in there," he told the Sheriff, "but you might get dirty."

I sat there holding my breath, sweating, feeling the heat as the brightest damn flashlight I have ever seen swept through the visible portion of the cubbyhole, missing my feet by only a centimeter or two. It felt like I was playing dead in plain sight, in the middle of the afternoon, and the longer they both stood there talking about what had happened, the more convinced I became that I was just fucked and that one of them was going to climb up on the porch to look inside. In fact, I find it impossible that right *then* they didn't see part of my shoe—some kind of freak miracle...

Their flashlights were so high-powered that the light reflecting off the ground and rails permeated the slits in the bottom of the train car and illuminated the inside of the cubbyhole like someone was standing right behind me. Hours passed in just those few weighted seconds, but slowly their lights faded, as did their voices and the scuffling of rocks as the Sheriffs gave up and returned to their vehicles. The Engineer then came back by on his way to the front of the train, stopping at the porch one last time to shine his light in. But I hadn't budged and nothing had changed. I imagined he sort of sighed and shook his head incredulously, and then walked on. I heard distant gravel crunching under tires once more, and I finally climbed out to see three vehicles descending the service road back down the mountain. By this time I could barely even see the DPU the fog was so thick. The train creaked slowly into motion with that experienced-Engineer's touch and quickly resumed its normal pace.

I had just survived a five-hour manhunt and was not taking any more chances. I scrunched my six-foot frame up in that four-foot by three-foot cubbyhole and stayed there throughout the rest of the cold night.

*

1730- Klamath Falls got its name the same as Spokane, from a falls on the river named after the Natives. Klamath, a name given by the White Man to the tribes that lived along the Williamson[5] and Sprague[6] Rivers, is derived from what the

Natives called the land—*Claminitt* or *Clammitte*[7]—and not their name for themselves—the *Eukshikni*, or *Auksni*, meaning "the People of the Lake,"—which did not prove Anglo-lexical-friendly. The falls was *Tiwishkeni*, or "Rush of Falling Waters Place," and being on a river that linked Upper Klamath Lake to the Klamath River, the town was originally called

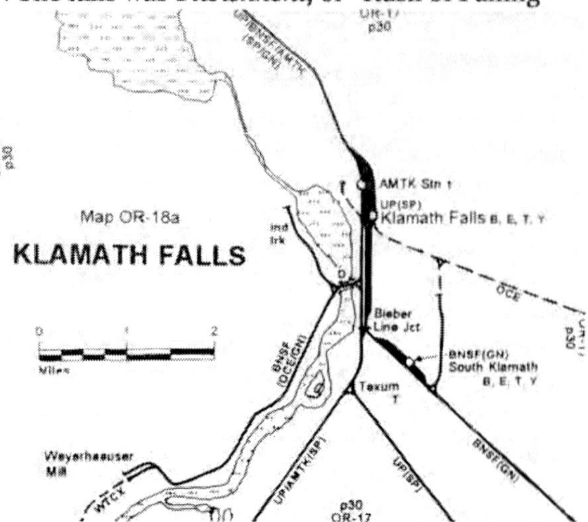

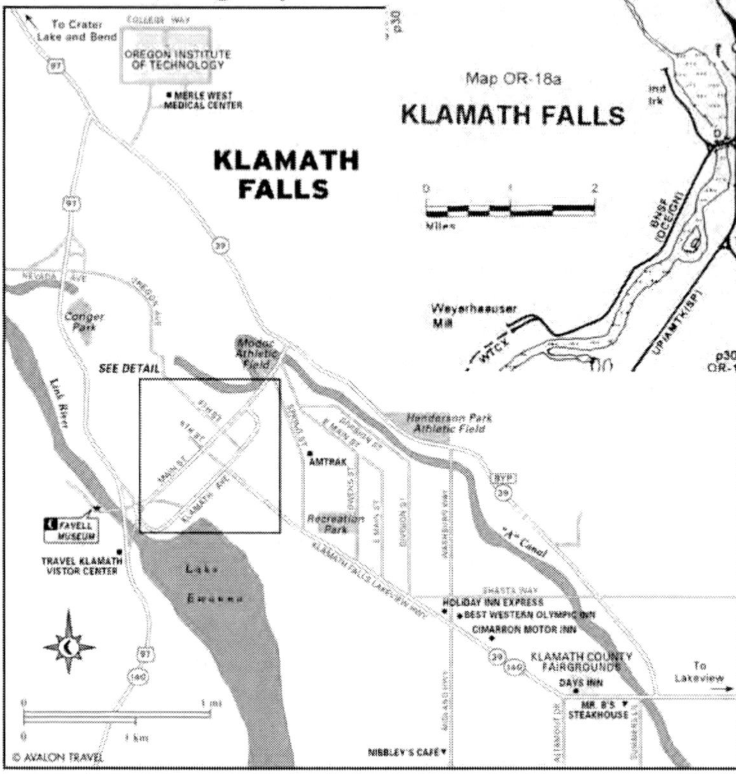

Linkville for the river Link. So yes, there is actually a falls that the town is named after, but it is not on the Klamath River. And while you can see a picture of it on the wall inside the Amtrak station here, I'm pretty sure it no longer exists in this era of dams.

The Klamath Basin is historically and ecologically a migratory marshland, one of the most important avian wildlife refuges in the Northern Hemisphere, and the Natives traditionally navigated it by canoe, hunting fowl and fishing. The town incorporated in the late 1800s after removal of the Natives to nearby (or not so nearby) reservations and much of the surrounding land was drained to make arable. The railroad arrived in 1911, and K-Falls became connected with Eugene and Bend by 1930.

Today the town is in good shape for its size, bustling and busy, and I'm receiv-

---

5. Named for Robert Stockton Williamson who explored parts of Central Oregon for the Pacific Railroad Surveys in 1855.

6. Named for Captain E.B. Sprague who was in command at Fort Klamath in 1866 during the Snake and Paiute Indian wars.

7. Possibly the native's adaptation of the French-fur-trader-used *clair metis*, meaning "light mist," as its often seen hovering above Upper Klamath Lake.

ing none of the profiling or hassle I expected. (Klamath County Sheriffs are known to be very hostile toward tramps and Railroad Bull history in Klamath Falls is particularly thick with lore[8]). But no, quite the opposite is happening rather. For one, the insanely nice people at the Green Blade Bakery did not let me leave without giving me some food for the road, which I of course accepted. I wasn't able to discern if they were a Christian business or not, but one woman, who could make just about any child seem chronically unhappy, told me how they just *love* traveling folk and likewise like to help them out. She hooked me up with a bag of ciabata rolls and a veggie sub sandwich. I spent an hour at the library before trying to locate a downtown railroad hobby shop that is no more, and then ran into a crusty couple that had just come down from Bend a few days ago and were headed to the Amtrak station to catch-out south.

me they had had no problems in K-Falls. I then walked to the south end of the UP yard to photograph the pillars under the 6th St. Bridge, and while nervous after what happened last night, I never encountered another, not even from a distance. Underneath the bridge is a flashback to the mid-to-late 90s, full of FTRA markings and some of the better-known hobos of that era. John Easley, for one, has at least two-dozen tags, all from different years throughout the 80s; and there are several old, full-scale Coaltrain drawings on the pillars. I walked around photographing for several hours, then laid down on my sleeping mat under the shade of a small birch tree and took a nap just outside the heat of the yard.

Klamath Falls yard: looking northwest

---

8. According to John Easley, the Bull in Klamath Falls was known as Roger Dodger, "because you had to *dodge* the motherfucker!" and was a generational Railroad Bull following in his father's footsteps.

Thanks: Crobar, Tone, Los Borrachos, Coaltrain, Read More Books, Herman Beans, Aware, Escape, Old Crow, Apel, Whisky, T-Box, Samara, Mishka, Lily, Tommy, Hoben, T. Erhler, Cam the Bikeman, April in Arcata, Norm, Lou, Walker, Robbie, Mike Diego, G-Bum, Liz and Fatty Natty, Mom and Pop, Morrises, Joe Biel, and BNSF and UP Railroads.

front half of train on opposite side of river

Cantara Loop

age and early-morning Autumn sunshine, the sounds and smells of everything instantly placing and distinguishable. The deciduous trees on the mountain shone a pastel yellow, preparing to drop leaves and go into winter hibernation, but the conifers still held their unchanging pine color, making for quite an overall contrast. At one point before rounding Cantara Loop, I could not only see across the river to our train pulling in the opposite direction, but could see from a greater height down onto the tops of boxcars from my same train going against the-DPU-I-was-in's direction. The train soon stopped to CC, and did so far enough back on the mainline that the I-5 arch-bridge was not yet in sight. Moving on, I did not see a single person in Dunsmuir. A northbound train sat waiting in the yard for clearance though, and the yard has not changed since I was here last (or the year before that).

South of Dunsmuir begins the Valley sub of UP's Roseville division. The tracks cling to the Upper Sacramento River's west bank, trying to keep up with its wild bends and tumbling descent. North of Dunsmuir the Sacramento is extremely secluded, a site for spiritual retreats and reclusive waterfalls; south of there the river is much more accessible and scenic, in a grandiose way. The river defines enormous wide turns around massive boulders, tumbles over craggy slants of rock, and at times narrows to a significant green depth squeezing through vertical granite columns. The train follows this course as best it can, but Mt. Shasta and the surrounding wilderness dictate that it straddle the river on multiple occasions; and in turn the land compromises by allowing itself to be delved through in those situations. A half dozen or so bridges cross the Sacramento to its east bank when necessary, and on most of those occasions a short tunnel through the hills follows. Like a rhythm, the train rolls across one 1901-built steel trestle, and a tunnel follows, which will then be followed by another bridge back

Sims siding

pulled into the hole at Judkins[33], a short, curved siding in a wooded area along the Willamette River on the eastern edge of town. This was the first time I have ever been on a train that has actually sided at Judkins, and because I have known them to *occasionally* crew-change there, and because there is a little pull-up area for cars to park right next to the tracks, I worried. Since we were not yet out of Eugene, we got off the unit and waited in the woods. A half-hour later a north-bound hotshot passed and we climbed back aboard the DPU. T-Box and I, confined in this engine's little cab together, were in for the long haul, and the train picked up speed through Springfield.

. . . steady climbing the loop up Coyote Mountain . . . T-Box throws his bag down, lays on the floor, and props his swollen ankle up on his bag. I'm in the Conductor's chair with my feet propped up on the dash, drinking my third High-Life of the night. There's a sound like the tuning fork of a guitar that just lingers in the air and then is suddenly ended by what sounds like the sharpening of a knife. There's the flange squealing off every curve, the train humming along at 20 mph up the mountain in the middle of the night, through tunnels, the noise pummeling off the walls back into the cab through soundproof windows and doors. And it's black all around . . .

*

The train pulled into K-Falls in the early A.M. acting strange: it stopped on the mainline before reaching the normal CC spot and then pulled down and stopped still further back from where it should have (considering the train was not that long), which meant that it had probably stopped before the Amtrak station to switch tracks and pull into the yard. The train then did just that; just what I did not want it to do. It was 3 A.M.

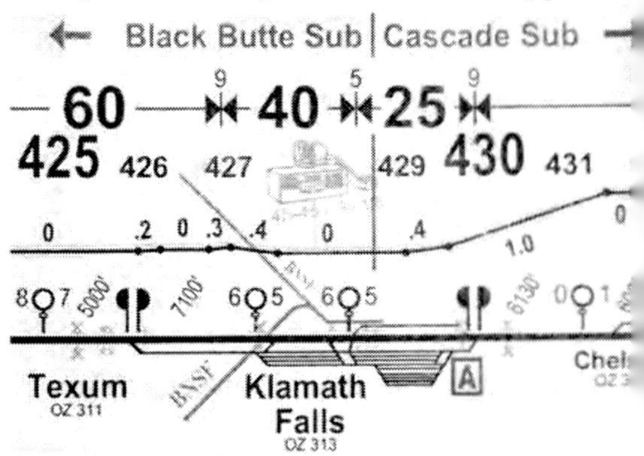

The train continued acting strange by pulling all the way down past the first bridge to the very south end of the yard, almost to where BNSF's tracks split east on their own yard-bound trajectory. For the next hour and a half we played a game of cat and mouse as workers came and went, drove up, stopped, and drove on, causing us to climb off, then back on, then hide our bags in the lavatory; and all the while the train continued acting strangely enough that I had no idea what it was doing. But no one ever actually came on board to inspect the unit and the train eventually rolled past Bieber Line Junction (BNSF's line southeast) and Texum[34] (UP's Modoc Northern line to Alturas, CA), and I fell back to sloom while still in Oregon.

South of South Mott, I woke to the train beginning its enormous descent into the Dunsmuir Canyon. I opened the Conductor's side window to sallow fall foli-

---

33. named for Thomas Judkins, an emigrant from New York who settled on a farm near there in 1853 (shortly after Eugene Skinner declared his nearby settlement Skinner's).

34. unknown

October, 2011

Eugene, OR- After scoping out the DPTs[32] and the yard and seeing that the regular nine-o'clock-southbound-working-on-the-first-industry-track train was not there, T-Box spotted some airplane-part cars connected to a line of some obscure rolling stock back in the yard (stuff that has no business staying in my area but is in high demand down in California), and what looked like a possible DPU, or two. It was a good call too. We waited strategically near a convenient store and our friend's house (because it was too cold to spend the night outdoors), underneath the Hwy in Washington-Jefferson Park, across the tracks from the basketball courts where all the skuzzards shelter. We had only been there about a half hour before I saw, flashing on the bushes next to me, a bright white light that got more and more intense like it was approaching. I put my beer aside and looked to see what it was, and sure enough two flashlights on bicycles were coming up the hill toward the pillar, zeroing in on us. But by the time I turned to alert T-Box one of them was already shining a flashlight—a heavy-duty, official one—all over the ground around him. Then, before I could even process who it was, the person extended his arm and offered T-Box some food. It turned out to be some Christian campus organization going around on bikes in the cold giving food to the homeless. They had seen our frames sitting against the pillars up under the bridge and peddled over in good faith to feed us. We each took a semi-warm, tin foil-wrapped bean & cheese burrito that T-Box later said tasted like it had no salt, and I thanked the kid real sincerely for the charity. Thirty-minutes later a train horn bleated through Van Buren crossing unmistakably—it was no Amtrak.

monving through Springfield, Oregon

With three lead units, a short row of airplane-part cars, Canadians, and at the end a couple of telling Golden West flats, the train came rolling at a quick-but-still-catchable speed on the secondary-mainline. T-Box caught the front ladder on the only DPU and was on it before I ever caught-on the back. I hustled down the walkway and tried to squeeze myself through the door before the train rolled through a crossing, but it wasn't until about a block later that I finally did. The train rolled gently through town and

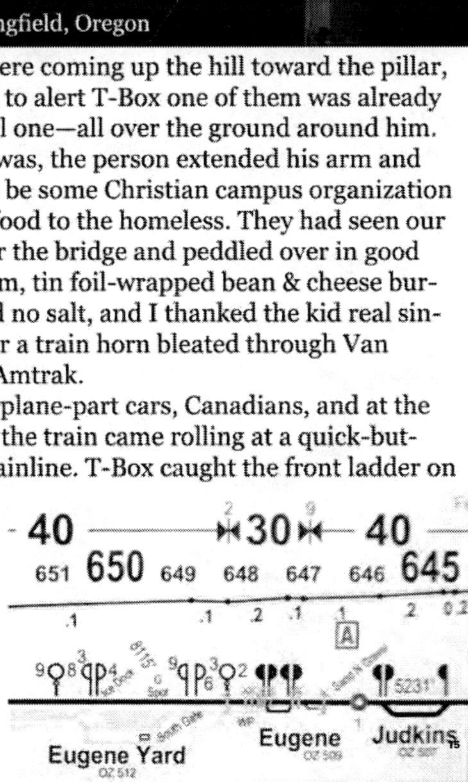

32. Departure Tracks.

Wash.-Jeff. Park Bridge Eugene, OR Oct. 2011

Pittsburgh, PA Oct. 2011[17]

five units back from the lead

speedometer facing the Conductor's chair said something like ERR. I guessed it safe to assume they wouldn't be coming back to check the fifth unit for any reason, and I laid out on the floor to sleep, the train climbing grades toward Crescent Lake in the Cascades.

I abruptly left the unit @ Dougren[29] in Pleasant Hill[30], not far from Springfield[31], when the train sided to let a southbound GM pass. I was on the catwalk pissing when I saw a flashlight coming back from the frontmost unit. The worker then came into the unit just in front of mine (which was facing the unit I was inside with its dome lights all ablaze). I watched him check the inspection card then turn toward me, and I ducked out of the way just before his headlamp shined in through the front windshield. He never came in but since I didn't know why he came back to check the inspection card in the first place, and because the first few cars on the line were two extra-tall airplane-part cars, I thought they might do something odd like break them off in Eugene, and so I got off the unit and walked back a dozen cars, climbed onto another loaded well-car, and rode into town in the dawn hours like I left Dunsmuir, sitting, drinking whiskey.

29. a combination of the name Douglas Green, who owned the land the railroad built on. Green wanted his named used for the siding being built but there was already one named that south of Roseburg, so they simply smashed his name together to get Dougren.

30. tis, and named such by Elijah Bristow, who staked his claim there in December 1847.

31. founded by the great and legendary Jebediah Springfield in 1849.

Dunsmuir, CA Sept. 2011

the daily Z-train approaches- Dunsmuir, CA

As the sun ducked behind the firred canyon walls shadowing the elongated little town of Dunsmuir, I knew I was in for a cold night, and I had a convincing change of heart about camping along the Upper Sacramento River being just two subs away (a night's run) from home. Riding north out of Dunsmuir, for me, has become routine anyhow.

Around 1945, just after nightfall, the daily Z-train, a hotshot to Portland that I have relied on like clockwork for the past few years, came screeching through the canyon with five lead units. Packed up and rearing to go, I climbed on the back end of a loaded well-car, sat on the grating as if I were squatting on a bench, took out my bottle of whiskey, and rode the train up through the darkened canyon watching the illuminating units strategically not far ahead. At North Azalea, the same siding where my southbound train stopped last time around, a southbound was appropriately sided and began to pull past as my train slowed to a crawl. Picking speed back up through Mt. Shasta the town, I laid my sleeping bag on the grating and looked up at the rotating globous of stars and the Milky Way band, clearly visible. I watched Ursa Major dodge back and forth on the western horizon in relation to the train, and I wondered where in it is said to be a "cosmic classic," a multi-billion-year-old supernova that peaked sometime just last week when its ancient light finally reached this miniscule planet; and somewheres SSE in the Las Vegas city lights Floyd Mayweather—undefeated—was fighting Victor Ortez for the welterweight championship belt (I've got my money on Mayweather).

ridin' double-stacks

I fell asleep to Klamath Falls, and when the train stopped to CC and I had the chance to go grab one of the front units (which I planned to), I balked. It was too nice out so I continued sleeping under the stars. Later, a little past Chemult, the train slowed onto a siding to let Amtrak pass south. Now too cold, and with an intensifying sore throat—the advent of which was germinated, no doubt, in the freezing spring-fed waters of the McCloud River—I packed everything up and hiked up to the first of the five front units, and made it just in time; the train began to pull forward as I squeezed down the catwalk and through the door. Inside, the unit was dead. The air was cold and the windows were open. Even the

Mt. Shasta looming

hallway. When I finally did see someone the next morning, she was walking her dog along the border of the yard as if the private property was now public domain and that was her morning routine. The McCloud River Lumber Company's plot too, a sectioned area east of McCloud that is almost as large as the very town, is entirely abandoned and unused. Hiking the tracks in, we explored football-field-size warehouses and juvenile-vandalized office buildings, roaming freely through what was once an important factory that sustained the railroad and the town itself.

*

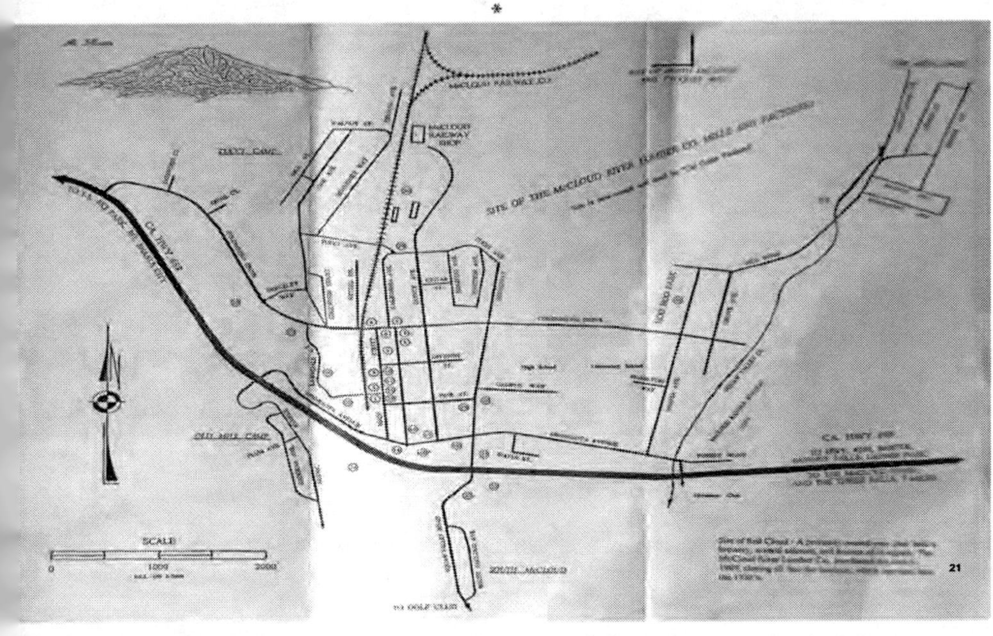

Me leaping from Upper McCloud Falls

[A High Sierra Explorer 55 travel pack that my brother gave to me for Christmas; an 8x8-foot blue tarp I found at a littered campsite behind REI along the UP mainline in Eugene and that I then took home and rinsed off; a brand-new Quadruple Dome T3 tent that I walked right out of said REI with just the other day and needed badly; a beaten-down, old gray Ridgerest sleeping mat that I can't recall from where I got but that I've traveled with for years and find a necessity for sleeping; a brand-new Zephyr 2 synthetic sleeping bag I got on credit from REI after exchanging my severely abused Mojave sleeping bag (a previous gift from a girlfriend) that had oil and grease stains, was torn and tied back up with twist ties, and was missing half its down while the remaining half was all clumped up from several attempts at washing; and a small white travel-pillow I took from an Amtrak train a couple of months ago. Six pairs of new socks (they go fast), four pairs of underwear, basketball shorts that were my brothers and that I now use for swimming and river-bathing, a pair of long corduroy pants that Sam got for me used from her friend in Seattle, a leather belt that I found on the tracks at the same place as the blue tarp and that surprisingly fit and on which I put my belt buckle of an old steam engine that Eli sent me some years ago for my birthday. Three t-shirts: a new, gray UP shirt I just got from the gift shop inside Union Station in Portland (for free), a hunter-green Sierra Nevada Celebration Ale shirt a library custodian in Arcata gave to me two-years ago and that I just recently sewed up a hole on, and a light-gray Louisville & Nashville Railroad shirt that Read got for me in Nashville a few weeks back. One thin, long-sleeve flannel that is Sam's but still somehow fits me. Six copies of Railroad Semantics #4 to give away along the way, a waterproof-packaged envelope for Brakeshoe containing Railroad Semantics issues #2, #3, and #4 to be thrown from the train when passing through Black Butte, four boxes of Markals (two dozen white, one dozen black, and a dozen assorted color Markals and lumber crayons); a Professional Railroad Atlas of North America (First Edition) that I got to replace the one I had stolen last summer in Martinez and that I purchased using an Amazon gift-card my younger brother gave for Christmas; a tattered, torn, and unbound copy of the 2000 CC Guide that I got from a friend who worked at Kinko's a long time ago and was just so happened to be asked to make a copy of it (and being punk rock and into trains and graffiti of course he did, make the copies, as well as a few extra for himself and friends); and Fog Charts of the Bend/Oregon Trunk, Cascade, Black Butte, and Valley Subdivisions. A black 2010 U.S. Census bag (the ones they gave to the homeless after tallying them) containing hair trimmers, a Coghlan's water filter, several UP crew-packs (paper towels, TP, and hand sanitizer), and three mini shampoo bottles from hotels. A zip-up bathroom bag containing a tube of fluoride toothpaste, a well-used toothbrush, Bee Flower Sandalwood soap (Rose), two bars of hotel soap, one reel of polyester thread (brown), a mini-sewing kit I bought for $3 at a gas station in Portland, three separate lighters, a box cutter, a straight razor, a (found) handyman, earplugs, two pair contact lens, a contacts case, contact fluid (half-full), FML Forte eye drops (for Carititis), Blistex, fifteen or so Q-tips, and toenail clippers. Two 33 oz. bottles of water. The Tracker, by Tom Wolfe, a book I bought for a friend but ended up not giving them (because they'd already read it) and that I decided to keep and try to read myself; Ken Kesey's Sometimes a Great Notion (which I am currently in the middle of reading); and a blank Gratitude Journal (sorry Tsunami). A three-triple-A-batteried headlamp, one yellow highlighter, a blue ink pen, one still functioning Justin Bieber doll, and a separate bag of food containing a loaf of Dave's Rye bread (expired), a jar of Marantha peanut butter and a jar of organic strawberry jelly, a plastic spoon (for spreading), half-eaten brown bread in tinfoil, a two day old burrito (made from leftover enchiladas Sam and I made), a bag of trail mix, two day-old garlic kale rolls, and a tub of garlic garbanzo bean dip. A black Nikon camera bag I got years ago with a Christmas gift card, containing a Nikon D-80 (weighted gift) with an 18-55mm vibration reduction lens, an 80-200mm lens I bought from my friend and former photo-editor, camera-battery charger, ACDC cord to transfer photos to computer, cell-phone and charger, a pair of gloves, my glasses, my wallet, dental floss, an extra contacts case, a green sharpie marker, Nanopod and headphones (another Christmas gift), pocket knife, lens caps for camera and lens, Olympus VN 7000 digital voice recorder ($15 on Amazon), two black and two white individual markals, drill bit, map of the State of Oregon, D-70 user-guide (my old camera), Union Pacific booklet of blank statements on track safety that I use sometimes for scrap paper, and several keys on a keychain with Big Sky Brewery bottle opener.]

Vandals push rocks onto train tracks

MADRAS — Railroad officials and central Oregon sheriff's detectives are trying to determine who pushed large boulders onto railroad tracks near a Madras trestle twice in recent weeks.

A freight train locomotive hit the first boulder and was damaged. Burlington Northern Santa Fe spokesman Gus Melonas said train conductors spotted the second boulder last week and stopped the train in time.

Autopsy: Man died before train hit car

BEND — An autopsy has determined that a Warm Springs man died of a broken neck in a rollover crash in Central Oregon that left a vehicle in the path of freight train.

The Bulletin reports that 21-year-old Paul Miller suffered the injury when he was ejected in the Saturday crash and died before the Burlington Northern train struck the vehicle.

Jefferson County sheriff's deputies say the driver of the car missed a corner and the vehicle rolled a couple of hundred feet before coming to rest on railroad tracks just outside the town of Metolius.

Two other passengers suffered minor injuries. Deputies have not released their names or identified the driver, saying the crash remains under investigation.

Man chasing dog is killed by train

A 47-year-old Oregon man has been killed in Eastern Washington after an Amtrak train struck him when he was chasing a hunting dog.

The Tri-City Herald reports the man was hunting with two other men about 10 miles east of Roosevelt, Klickitat County, on Friday morning when a hunting dog wandered toward the railroad tracks.

The man, from Bend, Ore., chased after the dog and he was hit.

The Benton County Sheriff's Office says it's unclear how the man was not aware of the oncoming train.

Bend hunter hit, killed by train

RICHLAND, Wash. — A 47-year-old Oregon man has been killed in eastern Washington after an Amtrak train struck him while he was chasing a hunting dog.

The man was hunting with two other men about 10 miles east of Roosevelt, Wash., on Friday morning when a hunting dog wandered toward the railroad tracks.

The man, who lived in Bend, chased after the dog, and he was hit.

Death laid to rollover, not train

By Lauren Dake
The Bulletin

The man who died in the car crash outside Metolius on Saturday was ejected from the car before the train hit the vehicle, according to the Jefferson County Sheriff's Office.

Paul Miller, 21, of Warm Springs, broke his neck in the car crash, an autopsy showed. The driver of the vehicle in which Miller was riding missed a corner on Eureka Lane. The car rolled a couple of hundred feet, hit some rocks and came to a stop on the railroad tracks.

"(Miller's) injuries were consistent with being thrown from a vehicle," Jefferson County Sheriff Jim Adkins said. "The train had nothing to do with the fatality."

Three other people were in the vehicle with Miller — a 31-year-old man from Warm Springs and a 30-year-old woman from Salem, both of whom suffered minor injuries, and a 22-year-old man from Warm Springs. Officials from the Jefferson County's Sheriff's Office declined to release the names of those people, saying the investigation is ongoing.

After the vehicle rolled, the female passenger ran to the nearby town of Metolius, about a half mile away, and called 911. While she was gone, and before emergency responders arrived, a northbound Burlington Northern train hit the car.

Police declined to say where the other occupants of the vehicle were when the train hit the car. Officials did say alcohol may have been a factor in the accident.

EUGENE

Man hit, killed by passing train

Eugene police say a 50-year-old man who walked in front of a slow-moving freight train was struck and killed.

Officers say the train was traveling about 25 mph Thursday afternoon and the rail crossing arms were down.

Sgt. Ron Tinseth says witnesses report the man waited for the train to get close, then stepped in front of it. One witness says the man was on crutches. The victim was not immediately identified.

with my back to the front of the well, ate my sandwich from the Green Blade Bakery, and read.

Building south from Bend in the early 1920s, Great Northern laid tracks through a site called Lava, an utterly alien landscape resulting from the prehistoric eruption of a Mount Mazama[13]-like volcano that covered Eastern Oregon with molten rock and left SSE of Bend a crater some 17 square-miles in diameter. The 1.2 million-year-ago eruption of the Newberry Volcano[14] left, much like Crater Lake, a single body of water in its collapsed caldera. But a million plus years of continued seismic activity and erosion forced a new uplift to emerge and now two lakes exist, one called East and the other named after an infamous, renegade Snake Indian Chief Paulina[15]. Surrounding this are cinder cones, deserts of obsidian, and a nine square-mile swath of crude black lava-rock suffocating 99% of the desert growth. I was entranced.

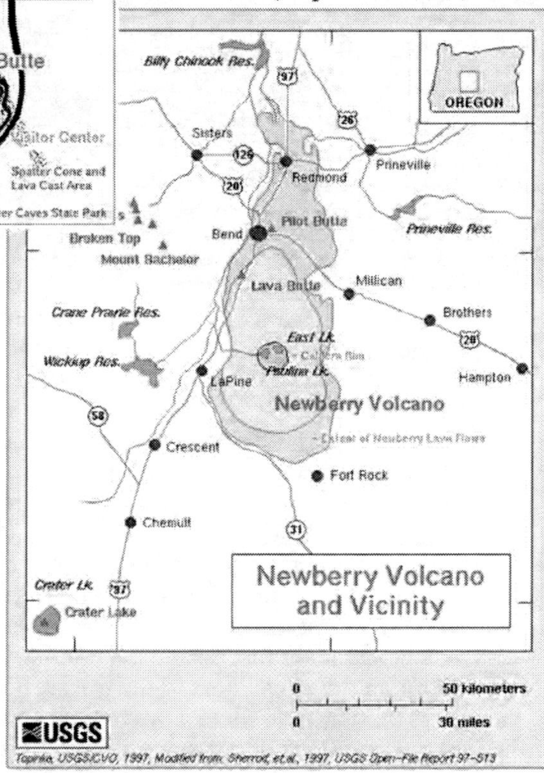

The sun had just set and the sky ahead appeared not the normal Earthly atmospheric blue, but more the color of a Martian sky—pink with a little bit of purple hue—and a waxing half-moon was on the rise just behind my visage standing on the grating at the front of the train car. Rolling through mounds of the lunar-looking rock, entirely void of any normal, natural elements, I felt, for those several miles, like I was riding a freight train on a foreign planet. And add to that the strange fashion of my creaking and clicking and clacking across the

13. The name of the mountain that erupted and collapsed into what today is Crater Lake.
14. of the mountains named for Dr. John Strong Newberry, a physician and naturalist who helped surveyed Central Oregon in 1855 for the Pacific Railroad Surveys.
15. spelled variously

Lava

land like I was, on a long, grinding, conveyer belt of steel. I breathed oxygen in deeply and exhaled carbon monoxide into the wind. The forest then returned as suddenly as it disappeared and minutes later the train stopped to change crews in Bend.

The CC in Bend is notoriously short, and perhaps why is that stretching back from the yard office, the length of the train blocks a road. I quickly climbed off, just beyond this crossing, where cars and bicyclists were in sight, and seconds later the train aired up and pulled off without me.

1300- Forrest told me that the best place to catch south from Bend is at Franklin St., where the tracks and Hwy 97 pass over. I am there, in the shade of the Les Schwab Tire Center, above the underpass, beside the tracks, and it smells like piss. I slept last night just beside the parking lot of this tire center with my tarp spread out on the gravel next to the tracks, not worrying about the morning because it is Sunday, and I had a dream that I went to a record store in Bend and bought the new Cephalic Carnage album. I dreamt this because the second-to-last time I was in Bend—the summer of '08—I went to Ranch Records downtown and bought a Cephalic Carnage album. (After coming across a Relapse Records compilation featuring an insanely good and remarkably evil-sounding Cephalic Carnage song, *Anomalies* became one of my favorite albums. However, *Xenosapien*, which I got in '08, was a significant letdown). So after remembering this very vivid dream I went to the same record store, and sure enough Cephalic Carnage had a new album out (well, new to me), and I got it (the first CD I've purchased in like two years). The downtown is actually only a short walk from where I slept, but I didn't know that this morning. Instead, I followed a spur track southeast toward the mountains thinking I'd hit some commerce. I did, but it was the wretched Old Mill District...

1645- Waiting for a train in Bend never did prove to be an active ordeal. Southbounds especially seem rare, and any consistency to their schedule I have yet to figure out. With today being Sunday and all, I expected it to be slow, but not even one train has come through since that northbound dropped me off last night, and *that* train didn't even leave until this morning.
1730- A northbound snuck up on and nearly clipped me while I was sitting in the shade on the railroad bridge. I vacated that spot for one further south along the tracks because I am afraid they'll call me in.
1923- Northbound GM with no DPU . . . *Goddamn your soul Stamper!* . . . Warm Radiant

Bend, OR- You could be waiting all day for a southbound train in Bend, as I have been since yesterday beforenoon. I waited in three different places: the Franklin St. underpass, beside a tractor in the Les Schwab parking lot (for shade), and, after dark, at Greenwood Ave., an underpass a little further north of Franklin where a couple train cars were laid up. But I ended up sleeping back down by Franklin St. on a little red loading-dock thing on the backside (trackside) of the Les Schwab building. A weak train horn jarred me awake around midnight (I'm guessing), but I could not tell if it was heading north or south. Soon though, a northbound came and pulled all the way down along the highway and clicked to a stop the same way as the empty well-cars the night before. This however was a general manifest, loaded, and with five or six lead units—a heavy train. My adrenaline levels spiked with another opportunity to ride north into the Deschutes River Canyon, but still half-asleep and low on supplies, I told myself to be patient, rest up more, and if the train was still there this morning then I'd seriously consider it but that ultimately I need to go south. A southbound did come through some A.M. hours later, but must've been terminating in the yard[16] because it blew furiously past without ever coming close to stopping.

This morning I woke with the sun and forced my crusted eyes open to see that the northbound had not budged. I walked to the store (Safeway is right up the street), got some more water, a little more food, and I'm now sitting next to a hopper waiting for the line to take off north. I'm pretty sure it's heading for Pasco, but I think I'll be able to catch off it on the fly at Fallbridge, before Wishram, if I don't first get the chance to climb aboard a southbound the train sides next to along the way, which has always happened when riding this line before.

from the loading dock

resting in front of well-cars

16. There is a small train yard in Bend a few miles south of the BNSF yard office, but I haven't been there before and it more than often looks empty when I've seen it passing by.

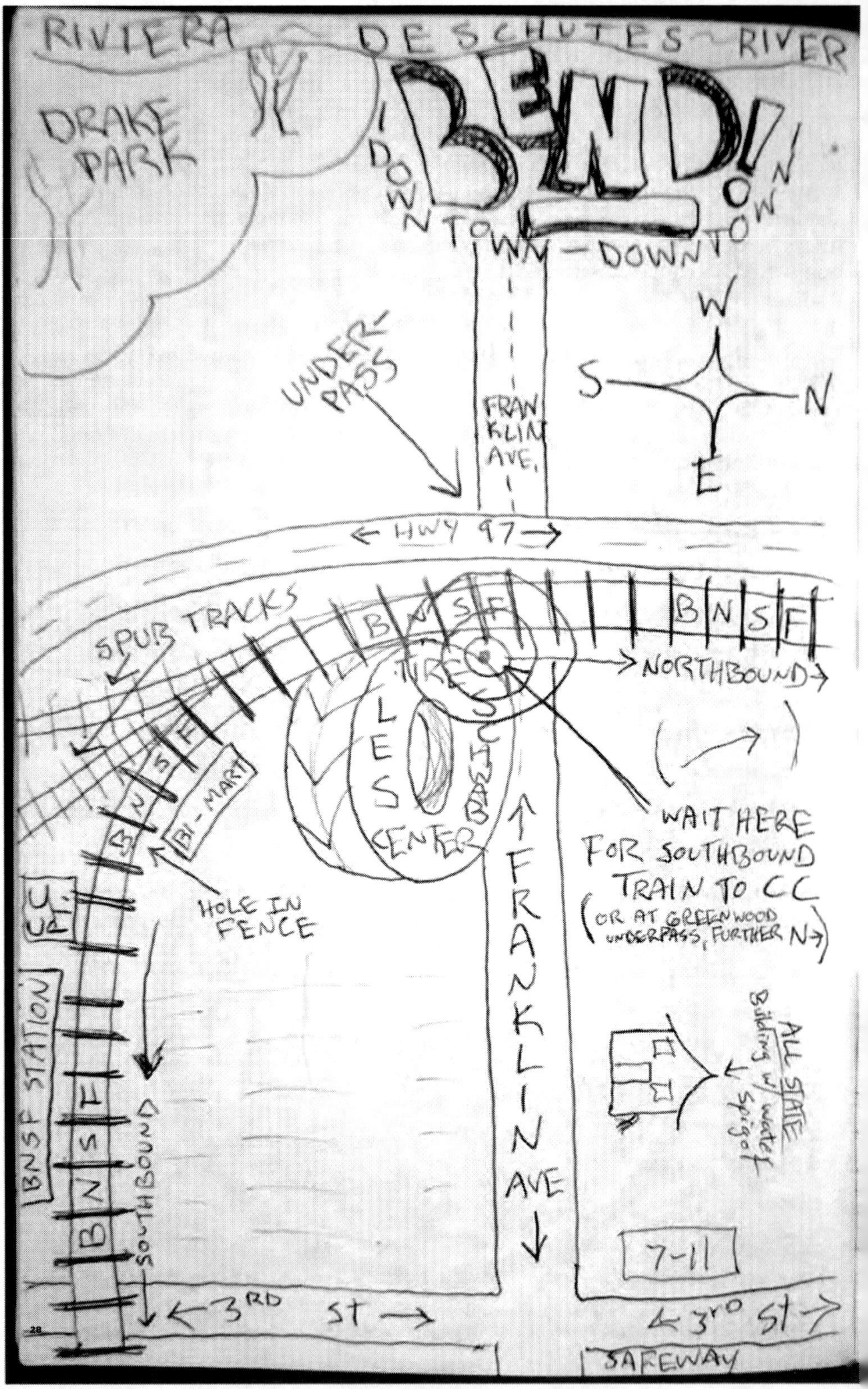
RIVIERA
DESCHUTES RIVER
DRAKE PARK
BEND!
DOWNTOWN
DOWNTOWN
W
S
N
E
UNDER-PASS
FRANKLIN AVE.
← HWY 97 →
SPUR TRACKS
BNSF
BNSF
NORTHBOUND →
LES SCHWAB TIRE CENTER
BI-MART
BNSF
HOLE IN FENCE
WAIT HERE FOR SOUTHBOUND TRAIN TO CC
(OR AT GREENWOOD UNDERPASS, FURTHER N→)
↑ FRANKLIN AVE ↓
ALL STATE Building w/ water spigot
BNSF STATION
BNSF
SOUTHBOUND
7-11
← 3RD ST →
← 3RD ST →
SAFEWAY

1000- The northbound from Bend was a no-go because here it still sits. Had it departed an hour ago—even a half-hour ago—I would have caught it north. But since I was waiting somewhere between Franklin and Greenwood on Railroad Property, I started to feel my own three-strike vulnerability. Then I got a call from my Arcata work-connection and they told me they could pick me up in the Bay on Wednesday (but Tuesday preferably), and so that means I need to catch-out of Bend today, get back down to K-Falls—no lollygagging—and then smash down to Roseville in one straight shot because they don't call it the Lost Coast for no reason[17].
1120- Northbound GM CCs at station, then stops on the mainline beside the other northbound GM, probably to drop off crew down at the other-northbound-GM's units. I walk in between the two lines for a brief minute or two before the GM on the mainline continues north.
1237- Well, after two southbound trains have passed, I'm still here. The other'n just came a rip-roarin' through without even a thought of stoppin' and I was left standing with my bags in hand like I'd just missed the last bus of the day. It's almost like they're just toyin' with me now.
1250- Now, finally, the northbound GM that pulled in almost twelve-hours ago says goodbye . . . *ain't nothin' for you to miss, Miss* . . . Foxtails season. Foxtails everywhere- in my socks, shoes, shirt . . . *the boogerin'!* . . .
1645- Another northbound GM. Sunny, cloudy, and cool after a half-hour nap.

1750- Along a dusty jeep path under the shade of a tree on the west side of the tracks behind the Bi-Mart building, lying amid bleached grass and knee-high foxtails... A line of empty well-cars pulled onto the siding beside the mainline. I refilled my water and got more beer. I may still go north yet...
2007- Sun set- I'm sitting on the RESTRICTED CLEARANCE loading dock on the backside of the Les Schwab building and it now smells oddly like macaroons. I am now 30-plus hours waiting for a train south in Bend and it's like waiting on a goddamn shortline. There have been plenty of opportunities to go north though, and the line of empty well-cars that pulled in a few hours ago is looking quite tempting to sleep on and ride to someplace else, particularly the front-end of those blue

17. The entire North Coast is not easy to access, but without a car you either have to hitchhike down from Crescent City (after getting *there* from Grants Pass, Oregon), hitchhike the 299 out of Redding (which you have to hitchhike *to* from Dunsmuir after riding the freight train there), or you have to go down to Martinez and then all the way back up the 101 via Amtrak bus or Greyhound.

BRAN 48" well-cars.

Ideally I'd catch a DPU south, fall asleep lightly under the flannel shirt I am wearing, and wake up in K-Falls by morning so I can get down to California in time. But I am losing confidence in that. Instead I'm thinking back to the two times I've hopped north out of Bend before (three if you count the two different trains T-Box and I took when we caught-off at Nena, camped for two nights, and then caught another train the rest of the way), and how both times the northbound train I was on stopped on the mainline beside a likewise sided southbound, and both trains were for several minutes at a standstill before either of them moved again. I'm thinking the probability is that that happens regularly on this line since it has so many slow orders, and so it seems likely I could just ride any old northbound out of Bend and then easily transfer to a southbound when the two trains side beside each other, rather than waiting here for another day. And if worse comes to worse I can just ride back to Vancouver, WA (since that's where this train's probably headed considering that's the most efficient route to the Sound's intermodal ports and these are all empty, waiting-to-be-filled well-cars) and catch a UP down from there (Portland, actually). I might even make better time at that anyway.

BRAN 48" well

2200- I must've packed and unpacked this bedroll 30 times in the last few days, but I guess it is a lot like opening and closing your bedroom door.

*

. . . the land is darker than the sky.

Oregon Trunk Junction- To catch south out of Bend I rode north. I fell asleep in the well of that empty BRAN 48" laid up along Hwy 97 in downtown Bend. The train took off before long and not too long after that I realized my hunch was correct: it is possible, and perhaps most reliable, to strategically catch south directly from a northbound train, climbing from one to the other when they eventually side parallel to each, which I have noted to be unique to this particular subdivision and nowhere else I've seen. Sure enough, sometime in the night (though I don't know where I was) my northbound sided next to a southbound and both trains sat motionless beside each other for at least a minute's time, maybe two. It was just what I was looking for to outsmart the Bend CC; the only problem was that I slept through it. I can't believe it either, that the engines on the other train, passing by so close to my head out in the open air, didn't even jar me awake because I sure as shit heard the DPU as it roared past! I knew my train had stopped though. I just had no idea it had sided beside another train. It wasn't until I heard the train quietly creak to life that I opened my eyes slightly and noticed the trees weren't moving in relation. That's when I realized it was another train I was hearing creak the ties and not my own. But at that point it was too late to pack up and catch the other train. I was somewhere in the canyon, and a darkness on the land so impenetrable made the glowing sky appear full of stars and unusually bright. The hills, cliffs, and loess-topped basalt rocks silhouetted unmistakably against the sky as I stood half-asleep in the warm desert air discerning the sight; onward I rolled.

It finally (re)occurred to me at the first hint of dawn—the canyon now opening up to its confluence with the mighty Columbia and the train rolling west on high basalt dikes toward Fallbridge—that I didn't have to go all the way back to Portland; I could instead catch off over the Columbia River where speed is limited by a slow order, and then probably catch back south from Washington soil. Then I remembered this old Coaltrain drawing I had years ago seen on one of the pillars underneath the Hwy on the Oregon side of the river, and how I wanted to get a photo of it. I thought that if he were there (and who the hell knows where else) it was bound to be at least a decent spot to camp; and so I caught-off the train at C.P. Celilo and walked up to the northern edge of Oregon and I looked out over UP's double-mainline Portland sub, the 4,197-foot-long Fallbridge that was constructed in 1910 over ancient Native fishing grounds, and watched the sun rise up from the vast Columbia River Gorge. And as soon as the sun rose the wind picked up magnanimously.

Here I stood at Celilo Falls, perhaps the single most important site in Oregon history, if not the entire Pacific Northwest. A series of horseshoe-shaped falls on the Columbia River, located 10-miles east of what is presently The Dalles[18],

Tunnel #1, westbound on the Columbia River Gorge

18. from the French *dalle* meaning "flagstone," "slab," or "spout for water," and that, for the Hudson Bay Co. fur-traders, described the rapids that flowed through deep, narrow chasms of river rock.

Tunnel #1; northbound on the Oregon Trunk sub

Tunnel #1; northbound on the Oregon Trunk sub

Celilo Falls was simply the best place in the solar system to fish Salmon.

Known as *Wyam* to the Natives, a word that means "echo of falling water" (an echo, one could say, of the graceful *Walama* used by the Kalapuyans to describe the falls on the Willamette), the origins of the name Celilo are unknown, but most likely came from the Se-li-lah tribe. The tribes that fished at Celilo[19]—the Chinooks in Oregon, Wascos and Wishrams in Washington—were some of the wealthiest and most respected, for Celilo was the longest continuously inhabited village in the Northern Hemisphere dating back ten-thousand years! What made Celilo Falls special was its commanding location on the largest, most powerful waterway west of the Rockies, the long sought after Northwest Passage.

The Oregonian/1933

The main cataract at Celilo Falls is seen in October 1933. The falls were flooded by the construction of The Dalles Dam in 1957, and rumor had it that the U.S. Army Corps of Engineers demolished them.

Long before its discovery the Columbia River was known to exist. Yet it remained elusive, the mythical River Ouragon[20] among early explorers. There is much lore surrounding the discovery of the Columbia, including that it was charted as early as the 1500s by Spain's Juan de Fuca, but it was not until 1792 that Captain Robert Gray and his ship Columbia Rediviva finally made their way through the turbulent eight-mile-wide Columbia Bar at Astoria Oregon and into the mouth of the river, which he then renamed for his vessel. 160 miles upstream from the river's mouth, situated at a place where it narrows and becomes constricted enough to essentially grasp, as far as its potential resources go, and a place that promptly required portage, Celilo Falls represented every major aspect important to the

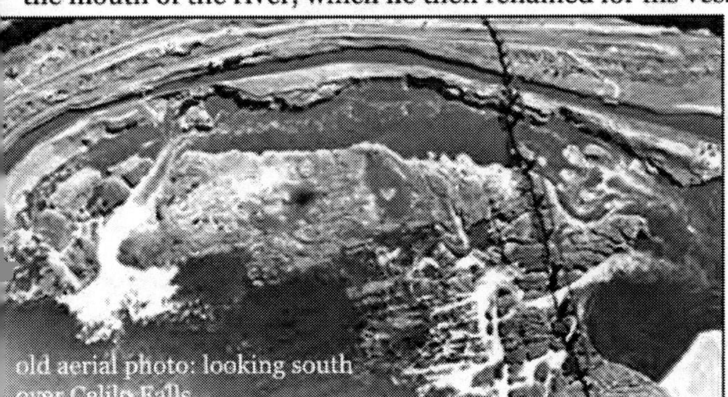

old aerial photo: looking south over Celilo Falls

19. also, it has been said, a Yakima Indian word meaning "cleft in the bank."
20. as it first appeared in writing in a 1765 petition by an English army officer to explore the land west of the Great Lakes. *Ouragon* is similar to *Aragon*, a term the French fur-traders used to denote the Spanish whose maps they often used. The Shoshoni Indians had a similar word they used to label their stomping ground: *Oyer'ungun*, meaning " the Land of Peace and Plenty."

Wide World Seen From Train Windows

STEPHANIE DIANI FOR THE NEW YORK TIMES

David Naylor, architectural historian, train buff.

AN architectural historian with a penchant for railroad stations, David Naylor has been traveling by train since the 1970s. He described the view from a train as a sort of movie, a documentary on the history of a region. "I would say that compared to the fragmented views out of car windows and the miniaturized views out of planes, the meditative view out of a train window is even better than television," he said.

Here are excerpts from conversations with Mr. Naylor about why and where to ride the rails.

RACHEL LEE HARRIS

Q. *Why travel by train?*

A. For me it is all about the window, watching the world pass by. You can just settle down into your seat, and the variety of the landscapes, even if you're passing through the worst industrial sections, is fascinating.

A. American trains offer a full range of vistas, like the majestic mountains near Puget Sound in the Northwest.

I plan to take the Pacific Surfliner in California, from Los Angeles to San Luis Obispo. We're lucky that some of these tracks were laid so early on that there wasn't anything else around. They got first dibs on the seasides

ON THE ROAD

Airlines Are Retrenching, And Alternatives Are Slim

Last year, Mr. Brown took trains round-trip from Minneapolis to Tampa, with stops in Chicago and Washington. "Yes, a long, long ride, but I loved every minute of it," he said.

Mr. Brown said the rail alternative could make sense on itineraries where the train was convenient even if time-consuming. With cutbacks that often require more connecting flights, and given the need to arrive at airports well before departure time, Mr. Brown says he often has to fly the day before a business meeting and "stay overnight if I'm to give my customers a full day of my consulting."

He added, "With Amtrak, I can often spend the night on the train instead of in a hotel room."

Ah, what a joy it would be if the trains in this country actually went to all the places we need to go. Since we're dreaming, let's add that it would be such a joy if the trains went there a lot faster, too — as in high-speed rail, which is usually defined as about 150 miles an hour or more.

Remember, my pleasant train trip from Tampa to New York City took 26 hours. Google Maps informs me that driving the same 1,125-mile route would take 19 and a half hours. The train is obviously more comfortable, but the fact is that the automobile goes faster, all things considered.

Alas, I predict 2012 will also be the year when we come to the collective realization that for the foreseeable future we may be stuck with the air, train and car transportation system as it is, given economics and politics.

undeveloped coast- McKinleville, CA

Today it opens at noon. I had planned to catch the Redwood Transit back into town but was stymied with the market being closed and couldn't get change. I stood in front of the bus stop with my thumb out and waited. I always feel foolish when I have my thumb out and an approaching car turns right in front me, or stops and goes no further, which is what one of the first cars that came by did. I smiled bashfully and put my thumb down. "What's all the smiling about?" a big beard screamed from the passenger window. By the looks of the man I thought him to be mentally ill or something. A few minutes later, the driver of that car hollered over, calling me Brother and asking me if I had seen a bus going north. I had not. The bus arrived a minute later and a man got off with a loaded little backpack and a tweeker-bike. There was some internal discussion and the driver of the car then hollered over that he would give me a ride. I accepted. The heckler with the beard gave up his front passenger seat to walk with the tweeker-bike guy, and I saw that he was not mentally retarded, just an age-old hippie who defies manners, though not generosity. As I moved to sit in his seat he reached in his little purse and gave me a huge, freshly trimmed and extremely fragrant bud. It was at least a couple grams of Green Crack. "You know what to do with this, right?"

The driver, an overweight, pale-white, fifty-some-odd-year-old with a dented nose and a car that looked as sloppy as he, was from around the area and told me that he used to be able to trim three pounds a day. He went out of his way to drop me off in McKinleyville so I could get change and catch a more-frequent bus to Arcata. I thanked him.

Willow Creek, CA- The bus ride here was $4 and jam-packed, but otherwise painless. I sat next to a longhaired, old hippy that looked like The Troll in Weaverville. But we didn't talk.

piercing through shadow that gave it the tiger-like striped appearance because now it looked more like a Lion! A few moments later I saw what it really was as it began to climb up toward the tracks at us: a large bobcat or mountain lion as big as a big human. We ran back into the trees and brush to hide and I quietly asked Aware if he had his bow and arrow with him. Luckily he did, but admitted that he didn't know if the arrow would be strong enough, or big enough, to pierce the beast; instead it may just anger the creature and alert it to our presence. I then grabbed my pack, darted further back into the trees, and hit the ground on my stomach, my vision momentarily fading to red, then black, and then returning as I remained lying there. Aware was on the ground too, a few feet away, with an arrow on a bowstring, aimed, and the string pulled taut. The bobcat was now up on the tracks, but still seemed to be unaware of us. However, it would only be a matter of time before it picked up our scent. I laid there motionless, silent, watching the beast pace the tracks back and forth with its head down, zigzagging toward us, closer and closer. I kept wishing Aware would just shoot it before it got too close, but he knew he only had one shot. The beast kept getting closer, too close for comfort, and in a second it all of a sudden stopped and sat directly in front of Aware with its back to him just a few feet away. We both kept silent and still. Suddenly, the beast's head snapped up at about fifteen-degrees to the left as if its senses had finally activated to the essence of human flesh. It turned then, and on its hind legs stood to face us, and in that single second that it stood there, staring for perhaps the first time into the face of a human being, Aware shot the arrow straight into its thick neck, piercing and protruding it. A coagulated glob of blood ballooned and oozed out the front of the neck and the creature fell, stunned, dead on sight. Once it hit I let out a loud, "Oh my God!" that probably woke everyone else in the house up.

1008- The Arcata Bay beaches are flat, lengthy expanses of sand a quarter mile from the 101 to the ocean, and the waves begin breaking another quarter-mile out, slow and long like miniature tsunamis. Just north of here, not five miles, the coast becomes rugged again, all jaggedy with rock, steep, and for the most part forested. Traveling south past a network of bays—Arcata Bay, Eureka Bay, Humboldt Bay—comes the Lost Coast, rough and even more secluded. But the portion I'm camped on, the succession of Clam Beach and Moonstone Beach, is relatively smooth and accessible, the sand strewn with seaweed that looks like large eels and bullwhips, or long taproot carrots, and some like rhino tusks. The water is frigid, and I let it wash over and engulf my feet while trying not to flinch at the sensation.

The Clam Beach Inn Market opens at 0900 everyday except Tuesday, today.

Trinidad, CA

McKinleyville, CA

August 2011

High in the Humboldt hills, deep in some German-named-river valley, outside a dim, unincorporated town . . . come look: the hysterical pluming of dust clouds as they rise into the air . . .

The first little disturbances, like miniature, dirt, A-bombs, erupting high into the sky, darkening out the sun. Then, settling slowly in the wake, on Douglas fir, poison oak, crow's feet and larf, coating every surface in a thick film of dirt, until the air clears enough to breath, and nature again stirs. Closer, the relentless patter of paws, a litter of nine German Shorthairs, a piglet, an interchanging population of man's-best-friends. Closer still, the imprinted treads of quads and four-wheelers, dirt bikes, off-road vehicles . . . and look: returning from river-bathing, transients from all over, again moving dirt, endlessly, day and night.

And for anyone else who might come and work.

dust plumes- Northern California

September 2011

McKinleyville, CA- *I went riding a train with Aware and some others. I don't remember who but it was somewhere through the Cascade Mountains, and at one point, at night, we were sort of sitting in the bushes waiting for another train to come back by the other way—it was just me and Aware at this point, the others were somewhere else. A couple of freeway overpasses and onramps were overlapping each other across from the tracks and from the railroad embankment you could look down upon these onramps all the way through to the shadowy pillars beneath. There, briefly passing under it all, stalking across the forest floor, I saw a tiger. A Fucking Tiger! I backed away cautiously to alert Aware, who immediately came over to look, and sure enough there the stalking animal was, lurking, unaware of our presence. But it must've been the slits of light*

Re: RR Semantics zines

Back to messages |

Brakeshoe 8/12/11

To Aaron Dactyl

Reply

Aaron,

You ain't gonna fucking believe what happened to your package. Day
before yesterday in the afternoon a couple friends and I were at our
place. The northbound RVPW had just been working the siding. We noticed
a Siskiyou County sheriff's department truck out talking to workers.
Soon more cops, the railroad bull and then UP officials from Dunsmuir
all showed up. I asked what was going on, they said there was a
suspicious package on the track reported by a worker, something wrapped
in black plastic. More people arrived. They locked down the whole area
for two hours, no trains were allowed to proceed through Black Butte.
Then the bomb squad showed up. They set up a dynamite charge on a
wire, and pulled the plunger --blowing up your zines! I asked later
what they have found and they said, "some railroad book with maps, it
must have been a railfan or rail rider." Fortunately, the label with my
name on it must have been turned down so they never saw it...but I found
a piece of tattered black plastic nearby with my name on it! Ha! It
seems none of them put 2 and 2 together and connected the package to our
place which is a good thing. In all it was pretty funny. But we still
don't have your zine (parts of it are scattered over a wide area.....).
Maybe next time you should just try the US postal service! 800 Black
Butte RD, Weed, CA 96094.

Bruce

the highway thirteen-miles from the Humboldt County line that is known as China Slide, after a massive landslide killed a large encampment of Chinese gold miners there during the 1800s. Remnants of the slide are clearly visible down on the northern bank of the river, where tons of cascading rock and landmass from the steep bank slid back up the other side of the mountain, temporarily damming the river.

Hwy 299, the Trinity Scenic Byway, is an exceptionally difficult road following the rugged Trinity River through largely uninhabited swaths of Shasta-Trinity

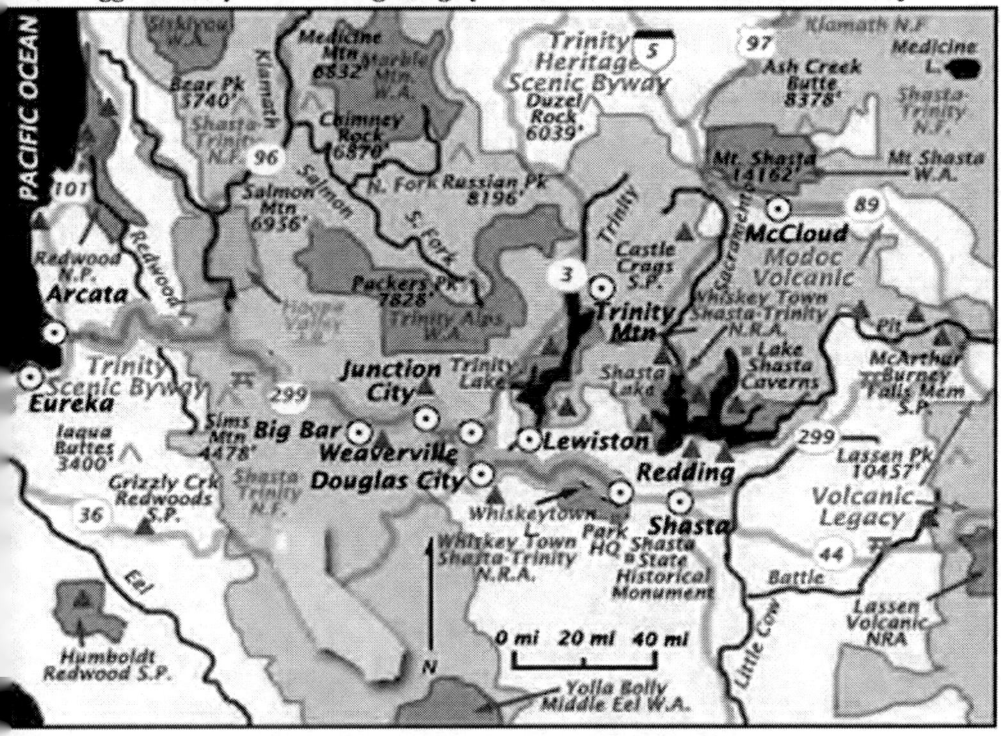

National Forest. This is the first time I've traveled it west. The mountains are steep to the degree you cannot feasibly hike them, and difficult enough that you would not want to be lost or alone in them for long. I imagined the original Forty Niners, hiking narrow creek beds and river canyons in by mule to the uncharted wilderness, homesteading here and there hoping to strike gold, fearful of the primitive Natives and a hairy, ten-foot-tall mythical creature with exceptionally large feet. A lot has changed in the outside world since the days gold mining ruled here, but deep in the mountains of the six rivers much remains a mystery and Big Foot is still thought to roam. My driver, for one, talks about Big Foot like its existence is a widely accepted fact, almost making me feel dumb for not believing. I questioned Big Foot's unprecedented elusiveness and asked, Why then do we not have some hard evidence that can be proven, like a body or bones? He answered that Big Foot's a humanoid and buries its' own. Still, the real reason behind my being unconvinced lies within the technology of motion sensors to trigger cameras. But I didn't bring that up. He's out there...

Canyon Creek, Junction City, CA

dropped me off told me that if I got bored to just jump in the river, and one look at this pure stream and I ran down under the bridge (a traveling-kids camping spot) stripped myself of clothes, and took my first bath in a week. The water wasn't even too cold, and was so clean-looking that I would've probably drunk straight from the stream if I had to. A million dollars later I stood across from the market in a fresh set of rags and in less than an hour had a ride from a big, red, diesel-burning pickup truck toting a rickety, heavy, flatbed trailer, and being driven by a 63-year-old man with a huge gut held in by suspenders who had a Mogwai-looking Chihuahua, piebald brown and white like a cow. He turned out to be quite an interesting accompaniment to the two-hour ride through Big Foot Country.

hitching America

Originally from Laytonville, he now lives in Leggett and is returning there from the property he just purchased in Junction City. He told me that he once hopped trains across Canada in the 1960s, going from Regina to Toronto to attend the World's Fair. Three weeks it took him and a friend, all the time in one of the front units with Conductor-consent. He said when they'd pull into a big yard, like Winnipeg, the Conductor'd tell him to get off and walk around to the other end of the yard and re-catch the train there. I asked him about staking claims along the Trinity River to mine for gold and it turns out he's done it. He actually worked Canyon Creek for two summers suction-dredging for five hours a day in a wet suit, and has worked claims on the Trinity as well. Altogether, he said he has mined a little over 20 ounces of gold, gold that he has not yet cashed in because the price is still rising. As a Californian, gold mining is very much his right, he believes. He more than once expressed his resentment for environmentalists who try to pass laws that ban suction-dredging, adding that he plans to sue the Federal Government be*cause* it is illegal right now. "They love their cell-phones and computers," he says about environmentalists, "but don't want the miners to do the work necessary to mine the gold for their phones." This may be true, but his strongest point to counter the environmentalist argument is that suction-dredging, while not harmful to fish, actually works to clean the river and get a lot of lead out, lead that is suctioned up in the form of fishing hooks and weights, and other discarded debris. He told me he used to get about ten-pounds of lead a week and that he'd melt it down to use as a belt-weight for his wet suit. As we drove along, he pointed out the cobble evidence that miners of old had worked particular parts of the river mining for gold. He also pointed out a section

piebald chihauhau

Arcata, CA- A wall of fog shrouds the coastline at sea, but in Arcata it's sunny and beautiful and full of street-kids and travelers. It took me a little over five hours and two rides to get here. I got my first ride west of Weaverville this morning after an hour-and-a-half waiting outside town. The youngish pickup-truck driver told me he had seen me on his way into Weaverville for supplies and told himself that if I were still there on his way back that he'd pick me up. He drove me over Oregon Mountain, through a pass in the Trinity Alps at 3,000-feet elevation where severe lightening-caused burns have raged thrice in the past ten years. It's obvious too as the road goes up and up

doess crossing the roa

looking east on Hwy 299

and up a grade I could not have continued walking. The road then suddenly careens wildly down the side of the mountain on an 8.5% decline straight into the facade of an enormous, burnt black-and-brown hillside of harsh, exposed rock-really fantastic! He dropped me off in Junction City, or just Junction: Population 16, the sign said. The driver told me someone always goes about tryin' to change the number when someone is born and that it really should read 216.

Junction City California is not a bad place to hitch out of. While it is the very definition of Podunk, it has a pretty good store and lots of people come through to fill up, get supplies, and pick up their mail at the tiny Post Office. They were nice in the store too, letting me fill my water bottle with no qualms, obviously used to people passing through. The best thing about getting dropped off in Junction City though is its adjacency to gold filled, clear water, Canyon Creek. The guy who

himself in to do twenty days for violating his no-drinking probation, and last night didn't sleep at all so that he could go to jail drunk and sleep as much time off as possible. But the jail didn't have his paper work and so they told him to go home and get it—home being his friend's trailer—and then come back. He is now going to The Diggin's to get a few games of Keno in first.

"I usually blow a 3.4 - 3.5—the Death Zone," he says laughing, gauging his blood-alcohol level like a driver does their speed.

Jeff tells me that after the first time he went to jail in Weaverville from drinking, that when he was released they gave him a check (not sure how reliable that is), and when he asked where he was supposed to cash the check they told him to cash it at The Diggin's. *What in the diggins is The Diggin's?* he thought. He then found The Diggin's and guess where he ended up the next night, again?

For all the times Jeff's been in jail it's only ever been drinking related, and the town's people and authori-ties alike, since they know him familiarly enough by name, do seem to generally like Jeff and are not trying to get rid of him. In that sense, putting Jeff in jail for drinking could be an authoritative act of kindness designed to save his life. On the other hand, 20 days sober behind bars is only going to throw the man into DTs so violent that equally harmful speed-like drugs will have to be dispensed to allev-iate it, which in turn is only going to transfer his dependency to something else. Like switching decks on the Titanic... the man is hopelessly incorrigible.

Jeff, the Weaverville town drunk

way out to the hills to work during the season, that reliable workers were hard to find. When he dropped me off he bought me two bottles of water—ice-cold—and I didn't object.

Main Street- Weaverville

Weaverville, CA- Weaverville is a quaint, old-fashioned town that reminds me of Willits the way the highway runs right through as Main Street. High school kids walk unchaperoned up and down the main strip in three- and four-person groups where there's a 1950s-esque hotdog stand, a market with a little diner inside, and an old movie theater still showing films. Except for some gas stations and a large-scale grocery-store area right when you come into town, the businesses are Mom-and-Pop independently owned and exist in old brick buildings that make getting onto almost any rooftop extra easy. Local drunks bumble up and down the street bumming smokes and sitting in front of several different bars, including The Diggin's, a local saloon-style tavern with a big, grizzled gold-miner on the sign overhead.

This morning I climbed off the rooftop I slept on and walked down a spiral wooden staircase to Main St. where I peered inside the window of a Natural Foods store to see when it might open. "You look lost," a man belched at me helpfully. He had a scruffy, graying red beard and long hair, an alcoholic's emaciation with a bit of a beer belly, and a black plastic bag holding a can of malt liquor. This is Jeff, the Weaverville town drunk, known locally as the Troll Under the Bridge for camping four-plus years under the Weaverville Creek Bridge below 299. When the Sheriff and California Highway Patrol (or simply CHP, as they are referred to by Jeff) eventually forcibly evicted him he stood there with a sign that read: Adopt A Troll. His gait is goofy, animated, and he accompanied me down the street to Susie's Bakery.

rooftop

"They messed up my plan," he told me, then explained. He was coming from the jail after checking

Eugene, OR- Eugene Skinner staked his land claim on the Willamette River in 1846 at the base of a coniferless butte the Natives called *Yapoah*. He built a cabin there, near a spring, moved his family in, and fifteen-years later died. That butte, now called Skinners, rises densely forested on the north side of downtown Eugene, along the base of which Union Pacific's tracks run. A replica of Skinner's log cabin stands along the river just down from where it was originally built[1] and Eugene Skinner can be seen staring stoically ahead, hat in hand, sitting on a bench in front of the Eugene Public Library.

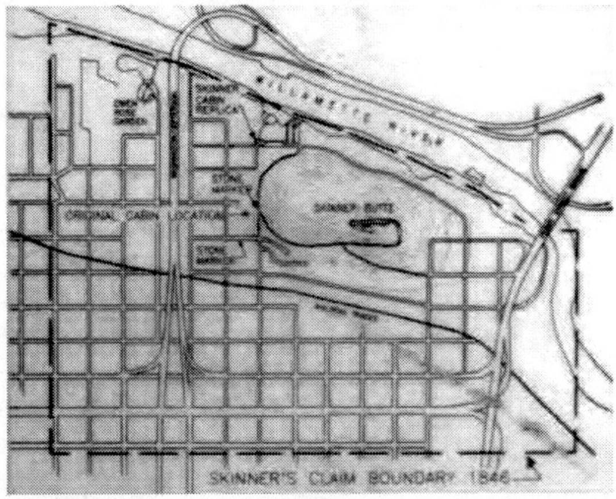

Following the discovery of gold in California, settlements quickly sprang up across the Willamette Valley, and with little resistance from the Natives due to the fact that they were, by this time, all but decimated by the white-mans' diseases (it seems as if this is how the Valley of Sickness, or Valley of Death, truly came to earn its name, not because of all the allergens in the air). With a donation land law enacted by Congress to encourage annexation of the Oregon Territory by giving free land to settlers, and with agriculture and timber industries on the rise, population grew rapid-ly. Statehood occurred in 1848 at the behest of Lincoln's Presidency, and Oregon City, with its prime location at Willamette Falls, was set to become Oregon's first major hub. Railroad construction in the Willamette Valley began soon after as a means to portage goods around the Falls and by the early 1870s rail lines reached Eugene under the guidance of a not-very-well-liked investor from Kentucky named Ben Holladay. The Oregon & California Railroad was then extended down through the Siskiyous into CA and by the early 1900s shortline branches and backwoods logging railroads had arterialized across the Valley.

Eugene Skinner

The inhabitation of today's Willamette Valley goes back many thousands of years, with the earliest Natives existing as mobile hunter-gatherer groups. Over time, these groups became more sedentary and storage-based as complex societies began to emerge along the many river valleys, developing language and customs, including rich oral histories detailing such epic events as the arrival of the first explorers (Spanish), the eruption of Mt. Mazama in 6,000 B.C., and even the great ice age Missoula Floods.

The Kalapuya[2] Indians, as the Natives came to be known, consisted of many bands grouped upon a similar regional dialect. An offshoot of general Salish, there was a certain intrinsic beauty in the Ka-

loess-topped basalt cliffs- Deschutes River Canyon

relocated onto the Warm Springs Reservation, I was struck by how lush and green the land appears compared to how stripped and barren is the Deschutes Canyon. But this makes perfect sense because, like with the Willamette Valley, the Missoula Floods carried rich sediment this far upriver and settled it, then slowly drained back out. This shows too as the land is also flatter in general.

The train stopped on the mainline around Redmond for a nerve-racking hour or so, then continued on unsteadily like it couldn't make up its mind to go. I saw tents and hobo camps along the tracks into Bend, and the train stopped right along Hwy 97 to crew-change, then continued south . . . *starting and stopping in the high-desert forest . . . sandy dirt paths running beside the train and the single mainline track . . . ponderosa and lodgepole pines, tall and thin and straight, some leaning onto others at canted angles . . . desert grasses and shrubs and lava ballast . . . tall straight trees of thin girth with not much of a canopy . . . a clearing in the forest with a barn . . . POS one mile: Check Your Authority . . . mile 30 Z . . . irrigation reservoirs . . . Klamath Mts. appearing . . . a road crossing with no cars . . . tires and trash and nothing for miles and miles . . . more dirt roads coming off a paved road . . . broken glass at the base of a tall tree . . . another road crossing—Finley Butte Rd—no cars . . . north Beal siding . . . log yard to the east . . . decimated forest surrounding . . .*

my bed in the DPU

*

Coming into Klamath Falls, swarms of insects hung in the air like clouds, and at first I thought they were sprinklers turned on. I climbed off two mid-line DPUs just after sunset and marched proudly up to the Safeway on Pine St. (downtown goes: Klamath, Main, and Pine, successively). I reupped on food, got a few cold beers, and returned to the catch-out spot where I had last seen Forrest and Roachel and sat on the remnants of their cardboard-box bed. It had been an epic day of non-stop train-riding that took me to the tip of Oregon and the Columbia River Gorge, straight down to the South Oregon border; from the gouged, volcanic interior of the remarkable Deschutes River Canyon, through the lush green valleys surrounding the Crooked River north of Bend, down the rural straightaway of high lava plains on the Columbia Intermontane, through sub-alpine forests to the Klamath Basin and Range. Twice in a single day I traversed the Oregon Trunk, my single most favorite subdivision and the very advent of my inexhaustible fascination with the Pacific Northwest; and not only did I ride freight through the entire canyon, but I did so in the utmost comfort of two mid-line DPUs on a beautifully sunny afternoon.

Lava (southbound)

Upper Klamath Lake sunset

Klamath Falls, OR- Amtrak sits at the station behind and I am down in the yard waiting aboard the DPU of a train I climbed on early this morning. A few curious things about it: first, the train didn't simply CC and then leave like usual, but rather rolled slowly through at catch-on-the-fly speed, so I followed it down past the Amtrak station and climbed on the DPU in the yard. But the side door was latched. *Oh shit!* I thought. *They're locking all DPUs now because of what happened in the mountains last week!* I thought I might have to climb in through a window and then found the front door to the cab open. But then a worker came on to inspect the unit, and I thought this to be the most curious thing because he didn't even really inspect the unit, he just walked through to see if anyone was aboard—any riders—and as far as I have known, units don't usually get inspected in K-Falls. Though the worker did check the inspection card, marking it at 0500, he must've just been a lazy worker because he wasn't in the unit for five seconds. But it's a good thing I saw him. I mean, the luck I sometimes have with these guys (and sometimes not). I had just climbed aboard and my stuff was kind of all over the cab (I hadn't even bothered to pack up my sleeping bag and sleeping mat after waking up), and I walk out onto the railing to look back over the yard and at a BNSF train that had just stopped on the mainline in front of me and I see some headlights coming down the road. Nothing out of the ordinary. But I wait for it to pass and it's one of those white Hertzberger suburbans, the crew-change vehicle, and it stops, right there across from the DPU-I'm-on with the BNSF train in between. Suddenly I see a light fluttering on the back of one of the BNSF train cars, like a worker is hooking up trains, and then I see a worker literally climbing across the coupler toward me and I say *Shit!* and dash back into the cab ahead of him (forgetting to relatch the side door) and just start grabbing shit and throwing it into the lavatory—sleeping bag, my entire pack, camera bag and all—and I run back out and grab my sleeping mat that I almost forgot and jump into the bathroom myself and, seriously, like two-seconds later I hear the door to the cab open and the worker walks in. It was brief, that's what struck me, like he was just passing through to look for someone. But he didn't even look in the lavatory. Five seconds was all it took and I hear him go out the front and shut the door with a heavy *clang!* and I just sit there breathing with "I'm just headed south" resting on my lips. (If they were only checking for riders, or really cared, they would have certainly checked the only hiding place in the DPU, right?) I fell back asleep after that and the train hasn't budged here in K-Falls.

Klamath Falls yard from the DPU, just before sunset

*

Lily pad moats and watersheds with pathways across them . . . the first hill gutted on the side with a hayfield next to it . . . Mt. Shasta visible on the horizon . . . more hay fields . . . a rolling hill that looks like a misplaced rock—a knob in the middle of nowhere covered with pine trees—a flat prairie-basin with a huge rock in the middle . . . the train curving west around the hills . . . Mt. Shasta glis-

tening on the horizon . . . cattle grazing in the drained basin below . . . Worden . . . elevation visually increasing . . . track work . . . an old silo . . . a tiny town with trailers where the tracks cross over a road and curve further west into the hills, then along more high farmland looking back over the Klamath Basin as the train climbs 1% grades and leaves the Hwy below . . . now curving back west . . . shrubs and very small trees growing out of the red-earth hillside . . . Mt. Shasta, ice-capped, looming physically over the farmland and back-country barns—wooden, traditionally shaped with brown planks . . . a 1909-built tunnel . . . exiting at mile 410 . . . red rocks and a sheer hill base of small pines . . . the tracks now curving to the west, skirting the hills—now California territory . . . tire marks in a dirt road beside the train tracks . . . the train climbing . . . veering slightly back east to level out . . . then veering wide left on a hillside of ponderosas . . . cattle standing scattered on pastures below with a creek running through and oval tracts, larger and larger, made on the pastureland like ripples in a pond . . . looking back on the hills and the train making a sort of u-turn . . . strikes from 7/10 . . . the Hwy going up over the tracks as the train goes into another tunnel, this one longer than the first but still less than a quarter-mile . . . emerging in Doris, a quaint little farming community with barns . . . crossing Gate, the main street there—a lumber supply shop, a little red shack with the number six painted on it . . . more lumber shacks and mills to the east of the train . . . a couple cars at each crossing and an old rusty water tower in a gravel lot . . . meadows . . . pasturelands . . . Mt. Shasta east . . . hay bales, horses, and further, endless rolling hills . . . grain silos and a new blacktop hwy carrying lots of car-carriers and semis . . . through Doris on a 0.1% grade, the train doing 49 of its 60 mph speed limit . . . desert shrubland on both sides of the train . . . occasionally a working farm . . . the land dotted with trees, the ground cracked, white, sand and mud . . . a little wooden cattle fence holding it all in . . . a thin layer of stratus hovering about halfway up the snowcap of Shasta . . . every 50-100 yards there is one tree large enough to provide shade on the parched desert . . . milepost 400: 78 miles from Dunsmuir; train doing 50 mph on a straightaway with no grade . . . farm machinery out to the east . . . Snot or something-Dell Lane . . . roadwork going on west of the train (they're ripping up and repaving the highway that runs alongside the tracks). Past that, it's nothing but that high California shrub-steppe . . . the train starting to curve west—Cheap Mt. Road, or something—to the western side of Shasta . . . sun-bleached grass growing up around a bunch of old machinery and trucks parked on the hill . . . aluminum tubing on the near-property that has some plywood shacks . . . two corrugated-metal barns . . . a bunch of barns . . . a bunch of wooden and corrugated-metal barns and a little town to

Mt. Shasta appearing on the horizon

Black Butte sub

. . . looking back over the Klamath Basin- Black Butte subdivision

the west with machinery and tractor parts in peoples' yards . . . Shasta now west and the train passing through a little farming community . . . hay baled . . . a big, half green field with trucks lined up at the edge—they look the type of trucks that carry tomatoes—and Shasta looming ahead brilliantly . . . the crops look like they're being watered, and I can't tell what the crops are—maybe strawberries—but there are people out, a tractor's parked in the field, and people are picking . . . now a freshly tilled field left fallow . . . Mount Hebron siding . . . grass seed, or something lush green, to the east of the train while the west side is the opposite of that—freshly plowed and colorless . . . the train now climbing, a mile or two past Hebron, on a 0.7% grade of track . . . more trees and less shrubbery, and less desert . . . distinct California trees . . . the hills encroaching and the train climbing . . . I can see the ridges and the ripples in the hills and the trees have that beetle problem that makes them all brown and dying—only about forty-percent of the trees are green . . . the other sixty-percent are decaying and you can see the dry hillside between their lifeless limbs all bare and spindly and burnt and white-limbed and black on the trunks like there happened years ago a burn . . . the tracks curving west and now curving back east and now back west again, snaking around Kegg on 1% grades, flange screeching . . . at the top of Kegg you can look back across the tops of the trees like you are looking over the clouds . . . and straight east is a mound of a million pine trees . . . the train cutting through rocky cliffs . . . milepost 384 . . . chugging up the grade at 28 mph . . . now back west and the flange squealing loudly . . . essing east. . . an old shack down in the shrubby valley . . . the train wrapping wildly around the western flank of the mountain . . . tons of junk, a couple of horses standing around, some trailers under a tree, and some shacks—someone's prime piece of homesteaded land on a shrub-steppe plot at the edge of a thin ponderosa forest . . . no farm to work though . . . the train climbing . . . 28's the speed . . . steep cliffsides to the west . . . looking across the valley, the train's noise echoing through canyons of

basalt . . . a junk yard/homestead east and the California-Stamper's are out collecting logs! . . . more of a cloud appearing to shroud the northwest face of Shasta, standing opposite a flat prairie with about a hundred head of cattle on probably thirty or forty acres . . . mile 381 . . . at eye level with a forest of thin ponderosas . . . hills undulating . . . Mt. Shasta clear off to the southeast and the train rounding its western base . . . a gravel road leading back to a trailer and a farm . . . the train curving strongly, wildly west, continuing up the grade, the bare, clear-cut Mountain in perfect view . . . across a zig-zagging stream—mile 379 . . . 33 mph . . . Penoyar siding to the west of the mainline and curves into a straightaway . . . red light visible ahead . . . highway reappearing brand-new and black and smelling of tar through a thin line of trees . . . mile 371: the

Coos Bay, Oregon

Eugene, and the yard is empty unlike I hoped it would be. There is nothing but a few caged-in ancients and a BNSF caboose on display, and an old gray passenger train. However, next door to the yard the Coos Bay Railway has its office, which looks new and promising, as there has been talk that this line is going to regain service. I can't wait.

Before coming here, I would have gone either way. Actually, I was hoping for a ride to Grants Pass, from which I would've hitched up the 5 to Winchester and tried to catch a train the rest of the way from there. Instead, a maniacal Irish-and-German Karuk Native driving a computer-chip-programmed pickup truck with boat in tow picked me up in Crescent City destined for The Mill Casino in Coos Bay. He was the type of guy who picks people up just to keep himself company and then spews to them the entire way. He told me about his newly-divorced wife and how he was giving her money each month to pay their vehicle insurance, but how when he recently went to get his boat licensed he found out that his truck had not been insured in almost a year! He then had to drive to Crescent City to re-register his truck because it has California Plates, or some variety of that mess. He cussed like an angry sailor, was vehement with rage at injustices and The Law, and overly opinionated about everything Native-related, which was just about everything. He was a full-on Conspiracy Theorist named Rick, from Happy Camp, and I had two and a half hours of his crazy UFO-encounter Big Foot-sighting Anti-Forest "Circus" (Service) rants/stories, and he did not let up the entire drive.

Hwy 101 in Southern Oregon- around Gold Beach

Hwy 101 in Southern Oregon- around Gold Beach

me of a story my friend Norm tells of when he once picked up a hitchhiker on the 101 in California. The Hitchhiker played the demo CD of his friend's rap group, some indie-rap blunt-smoking marijuana hip-hop that was so outrageous that Norm pleaded with, *begged* the Hitchhiker to let him have it, and it took the whole ride for him, Norm, to convince the Hitchhiker that it had been a life-changing experience, that the music so hit home with him he simply could not-COULD NOT—take the chance of never again hearing it; and so finally the Hitchhiker reneged, and on the basis of appreciative generosity he agreed to let Norm have the only copy of his friend's demo CD, something he very much prized, and Norm thanked him ever-so-gratefully, telling him he was so *so* glad that destiny had providently placed the Hitchhiker in his path that day (Norm can be really sincere and convincing at this kind of stuff and is known to put egregious amounts of money down on ridiculous, often self-humiliating bets, as well as ingest small frogs and any variety of amphibians for mere six-packs of beer); and so he dropped the Hitchhiker off with gracious extol and as the Hitchhiker was walking away Norm ejected the demo CD from the player, broke it into a dozen small pieces, and threw it out the window at the Hitchhiker for no reason at all other than that the music was *terrible*. Pelican Bay is nearby, so perhaps people are wary of picking up hitchhikers. I tilted my hat brim up more so people can see my eyes, but the sun's blinding. I wonder if I'll have to spend the night in Crescent City? As long as a cop doesn't stop me I won't give up. A red Corvette that looks like the Batmobile just drove by, as did a mail truck. I realigned my bag so it doesn't look as fat and bulky, but more linear. That may make a difference in getting picked up. The sun is behind thicker cirrus now. It's getting cold. My sweatshirt may have to come out. "Hitchhiking's *hard*," I heard a guy on the bus earlier say. I thought it was just hard for *him* because he was old. How come no one wants to pick up a kid? (That is what I consider myself while I still do this—a kid). An oil-tanker semi-truck that's front-end looks like a big-name country star's tour bus roars by. If I can just get to Grants Pass I'll be in good shape. I think I've been here long enough now that if I were going to get hassled by the highway patrol, I would have. Why, oh why, don't they have trains that come out here? I just noticed my new shoes are coming apart. My hoodie reeks. I'm not looking at these cars for likelies, I'm more just scanning the tops of and the shapes of them for CHPs. The front-left side of my right foot still feels like it's broken. Light is dimming. "Someone'll pick you up," they always say. A boat pulls over onto the shoulder. I am walking toward it.

Coos Bay, OR- Coos was the name of the Natives that lived here. Written as *Cook-koo-oose* by Lewis and Clark during their expedition, it is an Indian word[38] said to mean "place of pines," or perhaps "lake." Trains still are not running here from

maniac

38. also spelled Cahoos, Cowis, Cowes, Koo'as, Kowes, Koos, and Coose.

search me because I am on my way back from working and am hitchhiking with some clothes, books, and paint in a pack, my tent, sleeping bag, my camera in my camera bag, and about twelve-hundred dollars in cash. I've attacked the North Coast by about every other avenue before and I'm now trying this way to see if it's easier or quicker, but so far it's not and has instead been more expensive. I spent twenty-five dollars too much on a bus up here this morning, and a hideous bus ride it was, full of belligerent Indians saying "cuz" a lot and yelling ignorantly from the seat behind me about hunting. One of them had no teeth and another was freshly out of jail. I was more than glad to get off that bus, but I still got the feeling like *Fuck Crescent City* from the first moment I was here. It's cool out, and warming. I'm standing in a good place to get picked up but no one is stopping. A Police SUV just took the Washington Blvd exit but didn't do anything, yet. Two girls in a blue civic drove by and one of them gave me a thumbs up. People never stop if I'm willing them to, mentally, trying to make eye contact. It's almost always when I'm distracted by something it seems—when I least expect it. So I try to stay distracted to pass the time, hoping someone stops. But at the same time I've got to be on the lookout for the CHP—I don't want to put my thumb out to one of them. I must see *them* before they see me. I am standing on a gravelly shoulder next to a merging-lane on a newly paved, four-lane, 101/199 joint section of highway with about a three-lane-wide grass median in the middle. There's a bridge about a hundred yards ahead and signs trail back to it. The signs read as follow: Begin Freeway, Emergency Parking Only, Redwood Highway, When Flashing Traffic Info Tune Radio to 1610 AM, Traffic Laws Enforced By Aircraft, Speed Limit 65, Radar Enforced. There are two more signs I can't read and then another 65-mile-per-hour-speed-limit sign. On the opposite side of the street two high school girls walk against traffic while a long-boarder skates back down the highway with a plastic bag of gas-station goodies. The Long-boarder passes and turns and looks back at the girls asses. One of the girls wears wooly leather boots. A single-engine aircraft flies in low over the coast to the west. A shiny Victorian passes but I cannot tell if it is a taxicab or some other law-enforcement vehicle. I am aiming to get back to the I-5 corridor in Oregon by dark, and then figure things out from there. However, if someone did pick me up going up the 101 to Coos Bay or Florence, I'd take that ride. A U-Haul with two passengers honks at me and someone just gave me that I'm-only-going-a-short-way sign with the little pinchy fingers. A cop passes. He certainly knew I was hitchhiking even though I didn't have my thumb up. He may radio me in if he doesn't feel like doing the paper work. It's now bright again, the sun below the brim of my hat and warm on my front side. Some of these cars have their headlights on already. I wonder if people would stop for me easier if it were raining. Oceanfront Lodge Right On Main Street. It seems like every small town has a Main St. and like every coastal town has a Front St. Nothing is on the Hwy for thirty-seconds. I have less than half a bottle of water left. I wonder what are the chances of being picked up by someone who I know. I must've been passed by by at least a hundred north and northeastbound cars by now. I don't think a sign is very necessary on a road like this because it's all less than 100-mile distances with not much in between. There is no wrong way. If you get a ride, you are taking it. Considering the time, if I do make it to Grants Pass tonight, I may consider onramp hitchhiking because I'm anxious to get home, being about halfway there. A red jeep rolls past and reminds

and travelers of all kinds are strolling the streets, napping in the parks, and loitering downtown at the library and bus station. They spange in front of the Post Office, Kiva and Red Barn, camp under Chambers, Maxwell, and Beltline bridges, and under the overpass in Washington/Jefferson Park to wait for trains. Me? I'm at Chambers Bridge not entirely convinced on leaving today yet anxious to get out on my own and get a little bit more traveling in as I begin to make my way to California to work for the rest of the summer.

1400- I did not get the man's name. He came running up to me from a switch-train that was working the yard, panting and sweating and about forty-years old. With no pack and no water, he was clearly and alchy and a bum. He asked how to get to Portland on the train, said he and his buddy had caught a train down in Klamath Falls and got pulled off in Eugene by the Bull. He wasn't clear as to which type of car they got pulled off of (perhaps a gondola is what he described), but there were tickets and warrants and his friend went to jail. But he said the Bull was cool and told them he didn't mind if they rode; however, they'd been spotted and called in at some stop south of Springfield (perhaps by a passing Engineer looking down into a gondola?). I pointed him down the Northwest Hwy and told him to get some water at the market on North Park and to wait in the field there on the corner for a CC on the mainline. I told him to be patient—that a train will come.

1445- A train pulled into the yard from the south. A short train. Loaded. Possibly from Roseburg.

1635- A long train—the front half mainly woodchip cars and the back half mostly gray CN hoppers with mixed lumber racks and boxcars scattered in between—came from the south and pulled into the yard and stopped on one of the first three industry tracks. Fifteen-minutes later another train pulled in from the south, a loaded General Manifest with lumber from Douglas County (Roseburg area), and on it, the very same boxcar I rode down from Portland last Tuesday with Sam. It's just coming back up from Roseburg after being loaded.

1800- Some fifty-year-old Hispanic scumbag wearing a bandana and a skull t-shirt walked around the structure I was leaning against, mumbled something, and disappeared. A few minutes later he came back and asked if he could drink some of my water. I told him No, that it was all I had to get me so far south. He then mentioned something about Hollywood, saying that is where all his friends that are gay are, and then tried to explain that he wasn't gay but that growing up had been coerced into some incestuous diddling, and that he liked it. He was tweeked-out on something and if I hadn't already been ignoring him, I now certainly was. He continued talking as he walked away, then stopped on the tracks and hollered back something about a blowjob or wanting to give me one. I ignored the scumbag. Several minutes later he came back, this time with a hundred-pound lead, trackside object. I pulled my knife out and he

Eugene, OR Aug. 2011

lapuyan language, for it held a sense of poeticism that to this day is the reason so many Native words (though often blatantly bastardized) remain intact to name rivers, regions, and places. Joseph Gale, an early Oregon pioneer, remarked on this in the *Baker City Bed Rock Democrat* in 1875: "The Indians possess more poetic talent than we give them credit for; my reason for this is because I have witnessed many displays by them of that wonderful natural gift, a talent not taught them by proud sense, but naturally acquired. From being surrounded by the most magnificent work of nature; and from the sublimity of these, their souls are impressed, and will make use of language that would astonish those that are not acquainted with their manners and natural endowments."

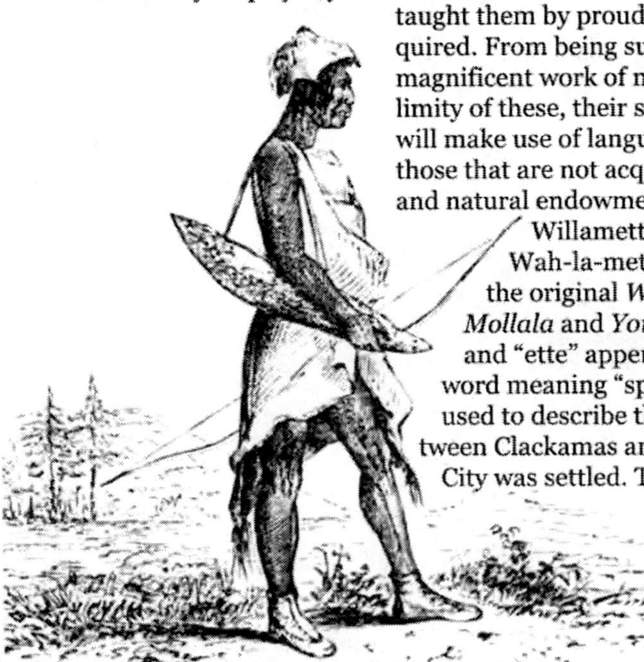
early illustration of a Kalapuyan

Willamette (correctly pronounced Wah-la-met) is a French adaptation of the original *Walama* (similar in sound to *Mollala* and *Yoncalla*) with the letters "et" and "ette" appendages. Walama then was a word meaning "spill water" that the Natives used to describe the section of the river be tween Clackamas and the Falls where Oregon City was settled. The river south of Clackamas[3] was referred to as *multnomah*[4], and Lewis and Clark, exploring the Columbia River and Oregon Territory in the early 1800s, then used the word "multnomah" to label the Natives living in that general vicinity, and *Walama*—or *Walamet*—assumed the name of the entire river, from its multiple sources in the Cascades to its confluence with the Columbia. Multnomah today denotes both a county and a major Cascadian waterfall in the state of Oregon, and *Walama* of course became Willamette.

August 2011

It's finally summer in Eugene: blackberries are ripe and ready for picking, bicyclists and pedestrians outnumber cars, the Willamette River features packs of half-naked people drifting on tubes and rafts, cluster after cluster, you can find a beer in the hand of one in three people any given time of day, and Kesey Square looks like a street-kid slumber party after dark. All around the living's easy and

---

1. what would today be 1st and Lincoln.
2. also *Calapooya* and *Calapooia*, and pronounced variously as "Col-lap-poh-yea-ass," "Call-law-poh-yea-as," and "Kala-pooyhas."
3. named after the Clackamas Indians that lived there.
4. a possible interpretive corruption of the Indian word *nemaltnomaq*, meaning "downriver," (which would have actually been upriver since the river flows north).

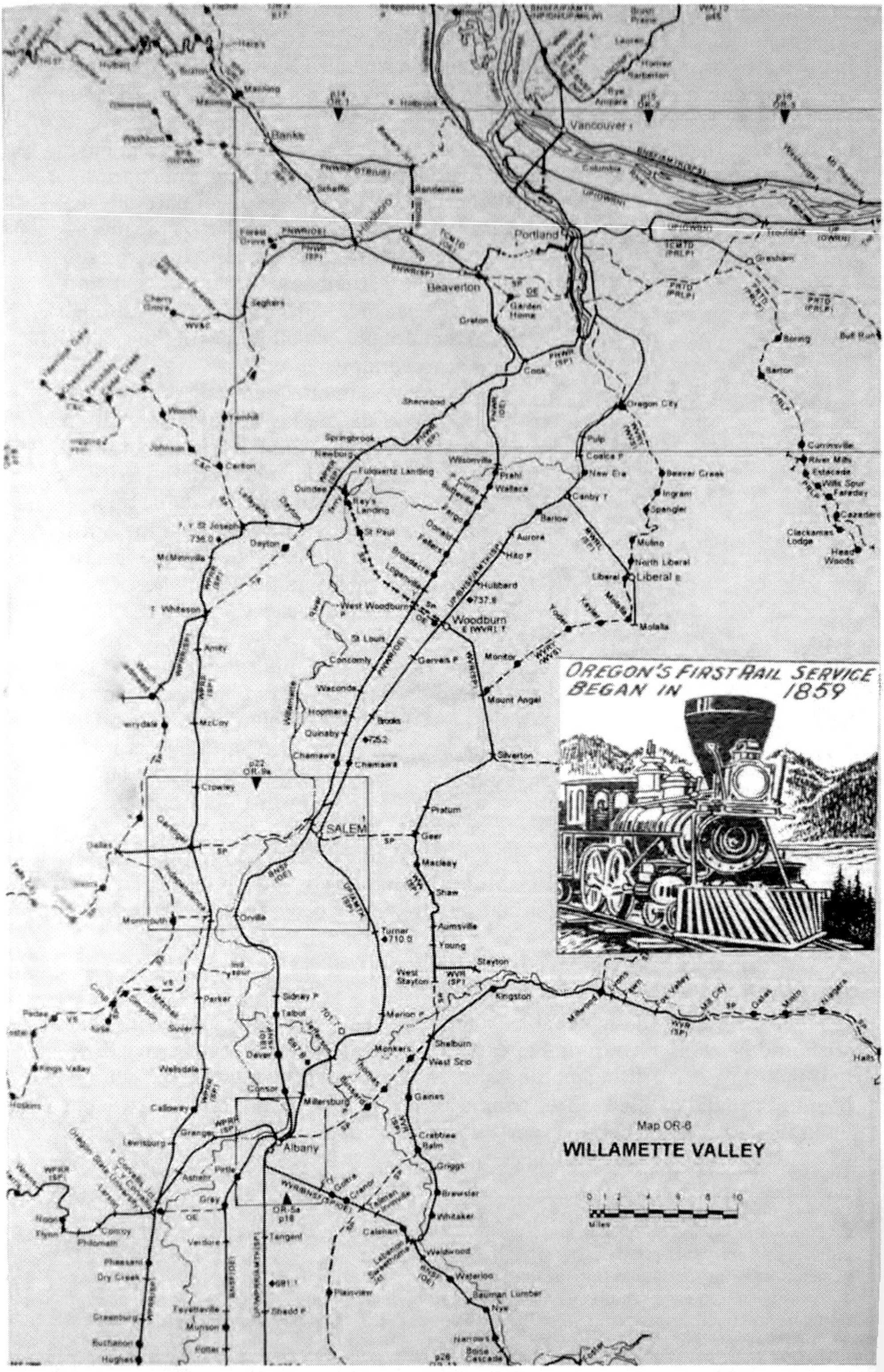

OREGON'S FIRST RAIL SERVICE
BEGAN IN 1859
Map OR-6
WILLAMETTE VALLEY
Miles
Vancouver
Portland
Beaverton
Banks
Forest Grove
Gresham
Oregon City
Sherwood
Springbrook
Newberg
Wilsonville
Canby
Aurora
Hubbard
Woodburn
Liberal
Molalla
Mount Angel
Silverton
Gervais
Brooks
Chemawa
SALEM
Turner
Aumsville
Stayton
West Stayton
Kingston
Shelburn
West Scio
Crabtree
Albany
Millersburg
Tangent
Lebanon
Sweet Home
Waterloo
Dallas
Monmouth
Orville
McMinnville
Dayton
Carlton
Yamhill
Amity
Whiteson
Philomath
Corvallis
Dundee
St Paul
Garden Home
Cook
Boring
Estacada
Lewisburg
Brownsville
Halsey
Sodaville
Dallas
SP
OE

summit . . . finally the train stops climbing, as is very noticeable from the sounds . . . there's no lake up here at Grass Lake, but there is a large valley of grass that looks like a lake, sort of. It's kind of flooded like a rice-paddy so I guess that's why they call it Grass Lake . . . the highway running right through it and the tracks are east of the highway and it's just a really flat expanse of waterlogged grass with a rest stop in between the lake of grass, all at over 4,000-feet elevation . . . a train sided up ahead . . . and . . . there goes the sided northbound curving away . . . [sound of train whizzing by] *. . . a standard manifest with some loaded autoracks, some reefers, a lot of empty lumber racks, and a lot of TBOXs (there was a worker back at the end of the line but I don't think he saw me) . . . mile 368 . . . tracks curving down through hills of dirt . . . Mt. Shasta appearing unbelievably large, dominating the east side of the train with its humungous north face . . . the train descending along its western base, an undulating landscape with a seriously undulating dirt road beside the tracks and that can only be handled by four-wheelers and dirt bikes . . . this just before Andesite, a siding snaking along the western edge of Shasta, which is completely in view east of the train . . . west is a rocky valley the tracks descend into where paths for bikes and four-wheelers are cut into rocks of all different subtle red shades with myriad green plants, lush and vibrant, from neon green to pond-scum green to pine green, all at knee-level with only a couple of trees poking above shoulder height . . . and Mt. Shasta just dominates the valley—it's magnificent! . . . the train wrapping even further westward and lava rock begins to appear . . . a tiny little dirt-road crossing . . . a little trestle over a concrete-runoff-colored stream that zigzags down to the valley . . . lava rock now covering the mountainside, dark, red and craggy, suffocating the land as the train cuts across it all . . . banana-looking plants on the edge of the tracks . . . 28 mph . . . slow rounding the bend (you've got to always be on the lookout for something around the bend) . . . the train snaking east then back west along this landscape of lava rock a lighter, reddish color than the lava rock outside of Bend . . . over a great trestle, crossing with squeaky cadence, high between the hills onto Hotlum, curving southeast around the base of Shasta and picking up speed . . . Black Butte coming into sight in the distance, as well as sand-colored mountains to the east a little snowcapped still . . . bags and buckets of spikes and plates line the rails as the train wraps down around Hotlum offering a view of Shasta's south face where there is less glacier . . . dead-end spur track . . . a round purple D sign . . . undulating dirt roads . . . remnants of some concrete buttressing structure . . . a dirt road crossing with no cars at the end of the siding . . . 28 mph approaching Black Butte, wrapping westward into a deep valley of trees and very steep dirt roads overlooking an equally steep ravine of*

Mt. Shasta

. . . crossing a great trestle

pines larger in height and more-nourished looking . . . lava rock covering the hillside, and looking west is a straight drop off to a valley of farmland that looks terraced the way that it's laid out . . . curving, screeching around the southwestern base of Shasta . . . scars in the landscape . . . missing trees . . . hills composed almost entirely of lava rock . . . curving back east and then snaking wildly west with Black Butte now very prominently ahead and the entire train again coming into view . . . passing a ridge of lava with Black Butte pointing up overtop. I can see the engines up front from all the way back here in the very last car, the DPU . . . curving westward along the base of the hill, Shasta's south face appears unbelievably clear out the back of the cab, taking up the entire windshield . . . (I've got some zines that the BBCRC has asked repeatedly for and as soon as I see the water tower at Black Butte siding I'm going to throw these water-proofed-packaged zines off the train) . . . the train shunting and hissing and slowing a little, rolling along . . . down over a dry creek bed . . . Black Butte standing tall, black, and proud ahead . . . (passing in front of the yellow Black Butte house, opposite the old wooden water tower, I threw the package, but into the wind so it did not travel far) . . . the highway passes over the tracks south of Black Butte and its pillars have been recently buffed so that there's no markings on them . . . heading toward snowy mountains that show more green and red as they come into view . . . 36 mph down the hill from Black Butte, looking out over campsites and homesteads that I can barely see through the passing trees . . . dirt roads . . . old-fashioned telephone wires . . . another road crossing . . . lots of shacks . . . crossing Deets road right before the tracks start to curve back east along the base of Black Butte—mile-342 . . . railroad signal and red light . . . Upton siding, unnaturally long, sitting straight out to the east of Shasta bordered by a gravel lot and some gravel industry and some torn up tracks . . . Black Butte now directly behind . . . paralleling a road and simultaneously

. . . looking straight back at Black Butte

. . . looking back at Mt. Shasta

lava rock in the foreground

crossing over the I-5 freeway, looking directly back at Black Butte centered perfectly . . . a castle-looking brick wall appearing along the road to the east . . . a guy on a motorcycle riding down the road with his red shirt flapping in the wind as the power lines seem to like hold in the train . . . another road crossing and then into Mt. Shasta the town . . . the train pulling off onto another track to avoid the yard, curving southeast like it's running on the same street as the cars . . . corrugated-metal buildings and propane tanks . . . the yard a mangle of spangled tracks that are all but empty except down by the far end where a couple of old boxcars sit—the same lumber racks and boxcars that have been sitting there for years, including a Prineville, OR boxcar with some bad graffiti on it—and Mt. Shasta in its mystical entirety looking down on this quaint little town like a statue . . . Alma street . . . more buildings and industries . . . Mile 336 . . . corrugated-tin-roof shacks . . . a guy dressed all in back walking the dirt path pushing a bicycle with a yellow flag on the back (he looks up briefly at the unit, but not intently enough to notice me) . . . screeching, curving westward around close-cropped pine trees . . . slowing to 31 mph with Shasta straight looming behind the train . . . a road crossing where a cement-truck and two cars wait, coming at an angle as the tracks cross in an eastward arc-curve . . . fairly nice homes on lush, bushy properties . . . a golf course to the right with a pond . . . the engine sighing and exhaling loudly . . . gazebos hiding back in the brush amid dense pine trees with limbs that sprawl out over and touch the ground . . . slowing drastically onto Azalea, a downgrade straightaway . . . slowing to 18 . . . now almost to a stop on this siding . . . yes, we are stopping, and I have stopped here before . . .

Redding, CA- It's 99 degrees in Redding. I got dropped off right on the I-5 shoulder by a Tibetan semi-truck-driver transporting paper bags to Los Angeles for NRI Vancouver, WA. He did not speak very good English, and while driving through the rugged Shasta terrain he head-signaled at the mountains posing his question as an answer: "No tigers?" I laughed as he then nodded now-knowingly. There are tigers all over the mountains where he comes from, he tells me. He then asks if there are snakes in Northern California and I give a casual Yes. His eyes get wide as he turns toward me with shock. "*Anaconda!?*" I laughed at his exuberant character.

Twice a week for four years now he has driven this I-5 route, often picking up

steep descent on Sawmill Curve

same train across the river- Dunsmuir Canyon

Dunsmuir, CA Aug. 2011

hitchhikers and sometimes giving them rides all the way. Once he saw, around Shasta Lake, a hit-by-a-car Black Bear. Little police sirens go off in his truck as a warning every time his speed inches above the legal limit. It's the first time I've ever been picked up by a semi-truck, and the grades up around Shasta Lake are tough on a rig.

Not five minutes after he drops me off on the shoulder in Redding, I am hiking up to the Lake Blvd. exit and a highway patrol is already behind me. You could've blindfolded me all the way from Houston, dropped me off on that damn highway, and with as quick as they were on top of me I'd be able to tell you that I must be in Redding. This motherfucker looked like that Vin Diesel guy too, and had a machine gun propped up between the two front seats of his very militant, black SUV. He drove me off the Hwy, ran my ID—an old Midwest non-drivers license due to expire in a few months but a valid ID none the less—and then peeled out without giving it back. It was the only ID I had left; all the others have been confiscated by the police for one dumb reason or another. (Ya, I forgot to ask for it back but forgive me, all I could think about was getting out of that cop car; and when I did he just sped off.) I found a bus stop, waited forty minutes, and I'm now on the bus going as far west from this red shithole as public-transitly possible.

crossing Shasta Lake on the freeway

I got the Tibetan-semi-truck-driver ride straight to Redding from Dunsmuir. I stood on the hot freeway for over an hour before he honked and pulled over unsafely onto the narrow shoulder. An hour before *that* I climbed off a DPU under the I-5 arch-bridge in Dunsmuir as the train CCed, and walked the tracks to the Amtrak Station to wash my hands, face, and hair. I was in town long enough to see that the Brown Trout Café is closed for remodeling. But the (new) manager over at the next-door store gave me a cup of hot coffee and told me how she's met some fine traveling kids in Dunsmuir. After speaking with her for a moment, I refilled my water and walked up to the Hwy to hitch. I was determined to get down to Redding in order to ramble as far west on the 299 as possible by dark and hopefully see a friend today on their birthday.

2020- Redding finally did me good and I got a ride out of there in like five minutes of being dropped off by the bus. (I figured Redding out this time: from the downtown bus center take the #2 and tell the driver you want to be dropped off as far west on 299 as RABA-possible, and that's like Eureka St., or something, right where 299 goes from being an inner-city commercial strip back to a two-lane highway, and there you can just walk west with a thumb out and not worry about getting hassled). A Grower of all people, a self-declared Emerald Triangle hermit from Trinity County[27] picked me up and drove me straight into Weaverville with his dog all nauseous and gagging in the back seat. The Grower was heading back down to Hayfork after probably dropping off some "weight" in Redding, and went the extra mile into town to help me out. He told me I was "good people" coming all the

27. with Humboldt and Mendocino being the two congruent sides.

COAL TRAIN

Fossil fuels make tracks through Oregon

Coal doesn't just burn hot, it burns dirty — it's pretty much dirt that burns — and like most hot things, it just might burn you.

No active commercial coal mines remain in Oregon, and the state plans to phase out coal from the Boardman coal-burning power plant in the Columbia Gorge by 2020. But if you thought coal wasn't a concern for Oregonians, think again. Oregon is pretty dependent on coal — almost 40 percent of the state's electricity comes from coal-burning power plants — and now Big Coal has plans to drive massive open trainloads of the grimy fossil fuel right through Eugene.

Coos Bay was once home to a coal mine and shipment of coal was a major part of its economy — almost one hundred years ago. But coal might be making a comeback in Coos Bay, and if it does, it will affect all of Lane County.

"I don't think people were prepared for it," says Grace Pettygrove, a Eugene activist who is organizing a coalition to fight the coal trains. She adds, "I think the Coos Bay proposal caught people off guard."

In October 2011, the Oregon International Port of Coos Bay signed an exclusive negotiating agreement with an anonymous company interested in shipping coal from the port. The code name for the coal export proposal is "Project Mainstay," and it calls for dredging the bay to deepen it, building a new terminal and shipping out of the port 6 to 10 million metric tons of coal a year. Estimates put that at one or two trains a day with 15,000 tons of coal — about 110 to 130 cars carrying 120 tons of coal each — coming from mines in Wyoming and Montana. Project Mainstay also means Eugene might see trains more than one mile long coming through town with huge amounts of coal dust blowing from the cars. A Sightline Institute investigation into coal found that "500 pounds to a ton of coal can escape from a single loaded car," according to calculations by the BNSF railroad.

Opponents point to multiple health issues including coal dust, diesel fumes blowing along the rail route, toxic pollution the coal burning in Asia will blow back to Oregon, contributions to climate change and a host of other problems that transporting coal will bring to local communities.

COAL EXPORT IN THE NORTHWEST

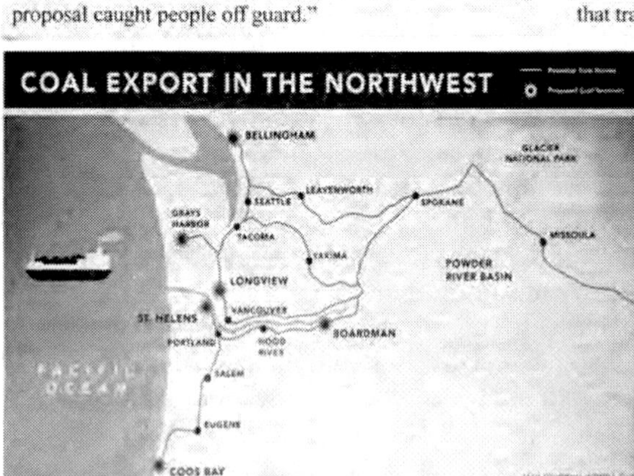

Theft, vandalism reported at rail line

The Oregon International Port of Coos Bay is offering a reward of up to $5,000 for the arrest and conviction of whoever was responsible for the theft of rail spikes on the Coos Bay rail line on or around Nov. 10.

Hundreds of rail spikes and tie plates on two segments of the tracks were stolen or damaged. The vandalism caused the minor derailment of one rail car and more than $20,000 in damage related to stolen materials and repairs, according to the Oregon International Port of Coos Bay.

Officials are asking anyone who has information on the theft and vandalism to contact the port office at 125 Central Ave., Suite 300, Coos Bay, or at 541-267-7678 or portcoos@portofcoosbay.com.

tween the two stalled lines, and crossed over to the river-side to look around. In less than five minutes my train inched on southward.

Coming around the bend at mile 63 I immediately recognized the landscape from when T-Box and I camped there almost two

BEND BRANCH

BNSF Oregon Trunk Subdivison

years ago[26]. The pictures I took then still convey the landscape perfectly as it has hardly changed—there was the giant boulder that I leapt from, the dirt path where we constructed our fire, and the fishing shack on the river where we napped. South from Nena to Redmond the line continues through no less stunning a landscape, following the canyon ten more miles south then crossing over to the east side of the river and going through a tunnel, the fourth tunnel from the Gorge. The train clings to the river's rugged east bank for ten *more* miles to South Junction, where the tracks then divert up the largely dried-out and now heavily farmed Trout Creek, crosses the Trout Creek Canyon, twice, enters into Tunnel 5, and then emerges and crosses back again to the west bank of the river. Continuing south through lush farm plots, the train crosses Willow Creek on an impressive trestle and then traverses the Crooked River 320 feet above a deep basalt canyon on a massive arch bridge spanning 420 feet across. With the Mutton Mountains west, where many of the Native Americans from Celilo were

Willow Creek trestle

26. see: *Railroad Semantics #2*

Railroad ordered to remove old ties

A complaint about the Deschutes riverbank prompts DEQ action

By Susan Palmer
The Register-Guard

Hundreds — perhaps thousands — of old creosote-soaked railroad ties dumped along a 30-mile stretch of the Deschutes River may be removed in coming months thanks to persistent cage-rattling by Eugene businessman and clean-water enthusiast John Brown.

Brown, a real estate broker, avid angler and commissioner with the Eugene Water & Electric Board, has spent the past five months complaining about the railroad ties to state officials and local and state politicians.

Brown's complaints bore fruit on March 1, when the state Department of Environmental Quality ordered the railroad owner, Burlington Northern and Santa Fe Railway, to remove the ties.

While steelhead fishing on the lower Deschutes last November, Brown had noticed the railroad ties on the west bank of the Central Oregon river.

Burlington Northern, one

Tom Penix/The Register-Guard

Continued from Page A1

of the nation's biggest railroads with 32,000 miles of track, owns the line that hugs the river through the spectacular Deschutes Canyon, a place that attracts thousands of anglers and boating enthusiasts each year.

Brown regularly fishes the Deschutes River, but it had been years since he had been on that particular stretch, a 30-mile run from the tiny town of Maupin down to South Junction.

"It's an incredible free-flowing glacial-fed river full of salmon, steelhead and wonderful native trout," and the last place you'd want to see junked railroad ties, Brown said.

Railroad ties are a crucial part of a railroad's structure, holding the rail lines in place. They're also highly toxic. The heavy wooden timbers are pressure-soaked in creosote to protect them from insects and weathering.

A derivative of coal tar, creosote contains hundreds of different chemicals, many of them polycyclic aromatic hydrocarbons. Some PAHs are toxic to aquatic organisms and designated as hazardous pollutants, said Suzana Radivojevic, a consultant with the Eugene-based Oregon Toxics Alliance.

The chemicals can leach out of the wood for years and into the water and can accumulate in sediments and plants, Radivojevic said. The leaching depends on many factors, such as the age of the wood, temperature and water flow rates, she said.

"Just the fact that there is an incredible number of waste ties which are potentially harmful to the environment does justify public concerns and calls

Ross Styles

Railroad ties *allegedly dumped by Burlington Northern Santa Fe Railway along the Deschutes.*

for their removal from the river," she said.

State and federal rules regulate the disposal of wood preserved with creosote. In general, railroads can store waste ties along their tracks temporarily, but not for longer than six months.

Earlier complaint in 1992

How long the ties have been there isn't clear.

Back in 1992, Bend resident Fred Boyle made the same complaint. Boyle, who had just retired as president of Central Oregon Community College, asked the railroad to clean up thousands of ties along the Deschutes, ties he said he had been looking at for 25 years as a fly fisherman.

Boyle made a videotape of the debris along the river, and wrote letters to then-Gov. Barbara Roberts and other state and federal officials, according to a Jan. 31, 1992, story in the Bend Bulletin newspaper. He asked that the cleanup be part of a management plan being written for the river.

canyon, the rapids are too severe to boat the entire river, and the canyon is so rugged and remote that the only ones that really get to see it all—from its mouth at the Columbia to where the tracks cross east of the river's flow and divert up Trout Creek (at South junction)—are the trains and the birds; and passenger trains don't come here anymore so it's limited to conductors and engineers, and hobos. It's kind of an odd paradox really, that it's actually easier (simpler and cheaper) to get to the Deschutes River Canyon via freight train than it is, or would be, to drive here, *or* hitchhike in. Upstream toward Bend where the river is tamer and more accessible, there is no canyon; downstream it's a different story entirely. The only way to get all the way through the canyon to the Columbia is

the view from the DPU looking back after exiting Tunnel #1:
eastbound on the Oregon Trunk sub

either get some wings or ride the rails.

The train kept to its speed-limit requirements, slowing to 10 mph between Moody[22] and Lockit[23], then again at Dike[24], and right before Nena[25]. Before reaching Nena however, the train stopped at Oakbrook, a 6,000-foot-long siding nestled on a 1%-incline of slightly curving track at mile 39. I've always sided there going through the canyon, and likewise a train going the opposite direction always seems to be sided there too; and that's exactly what happened this time. I saw the sided northbound ahead with its Conductor on the ground giving my train the appropriate "roll-by," and I ducked down until I was around the curve and out of view. My train then stopped and I got out briefly, walked in be-

22. named for Malcolm A. Moody, a pioneering resident of The Dalles who eventually served as a U.S. Representative in Congress.
23. Chinookan for four, as this was the fourth siding from the Columbia.
24. a word meaning "an embankment of earth constructed to hold water," and that aptly describes the track bed here.
25. a Native word, originally *nee-nee*, meaning "tall white cottonwood trees."

southbound- Deschutes River Canyon

North Crossing at Horseshoe Bend- Deschutes River Canyon

approaching Tunnel #1 eastbound on the Col. River Gorge

southbound in the Deschutes River Canyon

THE COLUMBIA RIVER BRIDGE

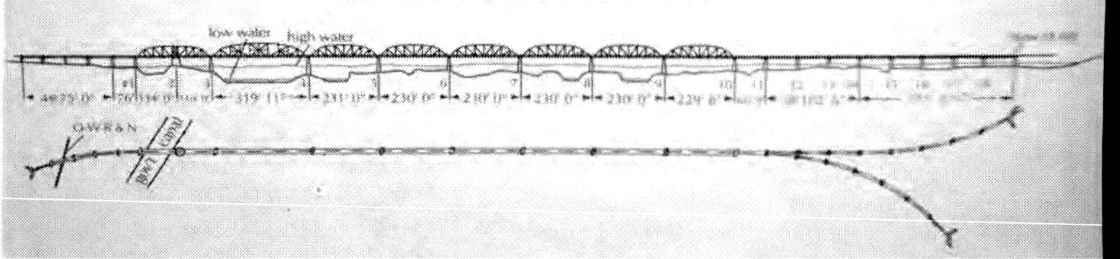

his presence known. From what I inferred he is Lonesome Walt, a teardrop insignia with 7-shaped facial features who's most likely a Native American from the Warm Springs Indian Reservation south of here, and perhaps a direct ancestor to the original Celilo Villagers. Below BNSF's tracks on the old Columbia River Gorge highway, a cracked concrete road overgrown with all manner of native fauna, I found Lonesome Walt's impressive camp. Though it did seem as if he would not mind having company (since he left a note on the metal trackside signal-box that declares it his homestead of thirty-five years with a little map drawn to mark where his camp is), it was mighty early and I did not want to disturb him or have a bunch of dogs barking at me, so I kept quiet and left him alone. But he's not hard to find it . . . *out here all alone it's comforting to be in a place where others have left their mark, knowing that their skeletons aren't just lying here decaying, that they caught-out ok . . . just seeing John's marking—it's like seeing an old friend. Even though it's just a drawing on a pillar, it's comforting. Unlike, say, at Ainsworth Jct. in Pasco where there wasn't a mark on the bridge, or in Wendover Wyoming, which was as abandoned a ghost town as I've ever been in. OT Jct. actually does get visitors and is a legitimate catch-out spot for trains south . . .*

*

I was not at Oregon Trunk Junction long. It is a forlorn place, yes, but I have been in much more lifeless forlorn places. And though I was tired, I was far too excited to rest. An hour into the sunrise I watched a long mixed freight train pull up to the bridge on the bright Washington shore. I knew it was coming my way. When the train got halfway across the bridge I noticed two mid-line DPUs toward the back end. I waited in the bushes as ready as I'll ever be and caught the DPU on the fly at about 10 mph. In morning sunlight I captured the Gorge in some of the most beautiful photographs I have taken all year. The train went through a medium-length archway through a stunning basalt plateau, and at the mouth of the Deschutes took south. In the deep river canyon it was still dawn.

I was at a loss for words. I thought about how lucky are the birds being able to perch in a high nest above one of the wildest, purest, most remote rivers in all the west, soar in low to the surface of the water then fly back up above it all, seeing for miles the path the canyon carves through the arid hills. But few can live here like the birds do. Man tries to conceive this landscape by vacationing here, fly-fishing, camping, boating and rafting—all of which you can do if you have the *means*. But few grasp it entirely. For me, the only way I'll ever get to experience this landscape is by freight train. But that's what makes it so unique: you can't just visit the Deschutes River Canyon like you can the Columbia River Gorge, and see it in its entirety. It's not that accessible. There are no roads the length of the

CALIFORNIA
WINTUN
8-30-1991
Nick TALLCAN
Buster
MUD
S.P.
STONE MAN
LONE SOME WALT
WARMSPRING OREGON
2-20-2006
HEAR
HOME STEDED
O.T. JUNCTION
"35 YEARS AND STILL HEAR"
DALLES
4-88
B. RICK
95
TOTAL MIND CONTROLL
Just Ed
9-02
DAKOTA
9-02
RUST BELT
7-10
KILROY WUZ HEAR
-054-2009
2010
96
TALLMAN
6-05
K-FALLS BOUND
TRAMP

Oregon Trunk Junction Aug. 2011

The Dalles Dam in the 1950s. The ancient village of Celilo has been lost too, first to the Government Canal (dredged in 1913), and then paved over and cut through by highway and railroad embankments. It's now quiet, deserted, and exists as a shell that everything runs right by, paying no mind to its history.

Before BNSF owned all the trackage rights here, James Hill's Great Northern operated the Oregon Trunk Railway, which is where the junction gets its name. But there is also a wye connecting BNSF's tracks to Union Pacific's which run

Oregon Trunk Junction

E/W along the gorge in Oregon, and that is the "junction" part of it. However, there's no station or anything here, just a signal box, and only under rare and very necessary circumstances does either railroad use the junction to access the other's trackage[21]. With The Dalles still miles away and no stores nearby, there really is no reason to stop at OT Jct. unless to catch back the other way, like I am. Nonetheless, there's a Coaltrain moniker on the pillar, larger than life and dating back to the 80s, and next to dozens of other recognizable monikers from the past couple of decades.

I was having sensory overload stalking around in the dawn light thinking about the significance of the Celilo site while processing the place as it now appeared to me: a rarely-visited catch-out spot and quasi-hobo jungle decades preserved yet threatened by construction projects, increasing isolation from society, and the overall decline in purpose—just out there, forgotten, and entirely uninhabited. Well almost...

OT Jct. does seem to have at least one full-time resident, a hobo-homesteader of sorts whose company I did not get the pleasure of but who nonetheless made

21. like for example the Frazier Landslide that obliterated the UP mainline for four months beginning January 2008 and caused many through-trains to be rerouted east to the Oregon Trunk.

region while centering around one thing: Salmon.

As an anadromous species, meaning they are born in freshwater (rivers) but live most of their lives in the ocean, then return to freshwater to reproduce, Salmon somehow instinctively know how and when to return to their home estuaries to spawn; and they do so by the millions, often migrating great distances. There are however, many obstacles in the way at this, and any fish destined for the great rivers and many tributaries upstream the Columbia from Celilo (the Snake, Deschutes, John Day, Salmon, etc.) had no choice but to navigate the roaring falls there, which, considering parts of the falls are upwards of forty-feet at

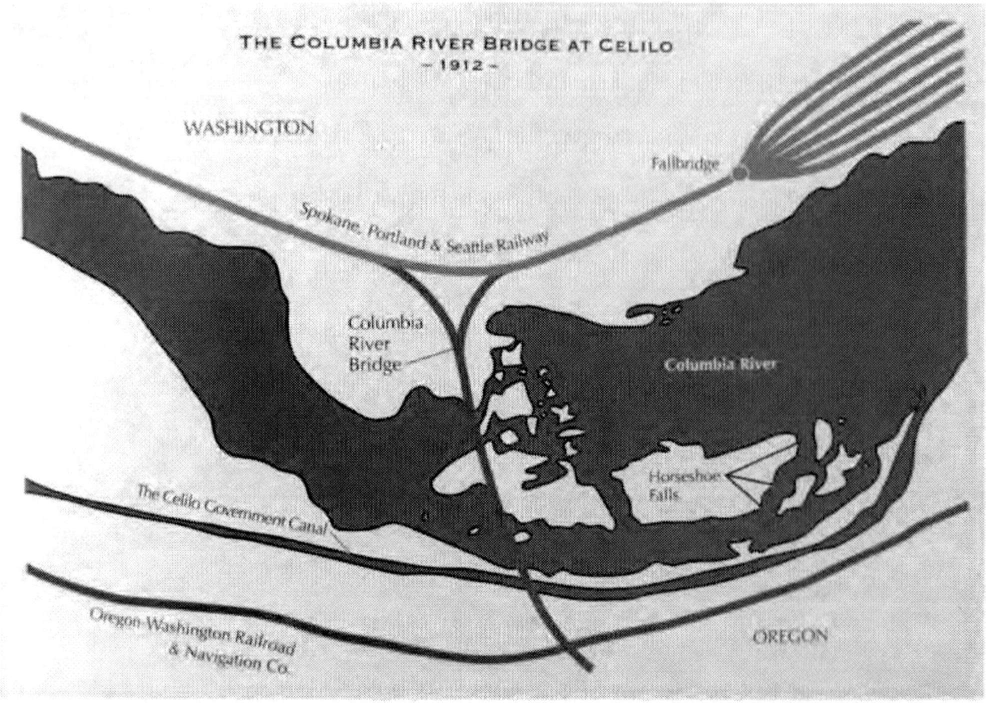

times, was no easy feat for a fish. Naturally, as Salmon evolved into great jumpers in order to conquer such obstructions, the Natives took advantage, learning to fish with dip-nets and spears; and while there are a multitude of Salmon-rich falls in the Pacific Northwest, (Willamette Falls, Spokane Falls, and Klamath Falls for example), the biggest and best Salmon were caught at Celilo due to its proximity to the Pacific at the forefront of the greater-Columbia watershed; and as Salmon runs were known to be predictable, occurring bi-annually on the Columbia, Salmon became the single most important regional resource and Natives from all over came to trade other regional goods for the rights to fish there during spawning season, which in turn made Celilo the central hub for commerce in the Pacific Northwest.

*

Oregon Trunk Junction exists entirely under the new Columbia River Gorge Highway as a series of underpasses, bridges, and abandoned roads and tracks overlapping, connecting, and crisscrossing. It is always in shadow. The sacred fishing grounds of Celilo Falls currently exist underwater due to the building of

Group focuses on train pollution

Idling locomotives in the Eugene rail yard raise health concerns

BY DIANE DIETZ
The Register-Guard

To Trainsong Neighborhood resident Jim Tiley, the difference is stark.

It's one shiny new locomotive on the Eugene rail yard tracks sitting next to another locomotive that's half-blackened, he said.

New locomotives are fitted with pollution control devices and anti-idling equipment. But an old puffer may sit idling on the tracks — putting out diesel smoke that's laden with toxic-bearing particulate, according to a report by the Lane Regional Air Protection Agency.

BRIAN DAVIES/The Register-Guard

A diesel engine *moves through the Union Pacific rail yard near the Trainsong neighborhood Tuesday in northwest Eugene.*

"I've been reading about diesel particulates and how nasty they are," said Tiley, who lives a half-block from the tracks. "When you see there are things that can be done, you start to ask questions about why they haven't."

In the next couple of weeks, a group of Eugene government, political and environmental leaders are planning to meet with Union Pacific about locomotive idling in the Eugene rail yard, which is on the north side of the city between Highway 99 and the Northwest Expressway.

The purpose is to find out

Turn to **TRAINS,** *Page B6*

Trains: Group will study ways to reduce toxic emissions

Continued from Page B1

how much time locomotives in the freight yard spend idling, what emission controls those locomotives have and whether there's additional technology, if any, that Union Pacific could employ to reduce the amount of particulate going into the Trainsong Neighborhood, according to Brenda Wilson, the Eugene intergovernmental affairs manager.

Union Pacific wants "to provide us with any information that we think we need. They're willing to sit down and talk with us face to face," she said.

Locomotives emit 53 tons of particulate in Lane County each year, the LRAPA report said.

Reducing diesel emissions is a major focus of LRAPA locally and the Environmental Protection Agency nationally because breathing the fine particulate in diesel smoke is a known hazard to human health.

The locomotives stationed at the Eugene freight yard are called "switch" locomotives because they're used to hook up and move cars from train-to-train to alter the cars' destination, Union Pacific spokesman Aaron Hunt said. Citing "competitive reasons," Hunt, who is based in Roseville, Calif., declined to say how many switch locomotives are stationed in Eugene.

But there are some reasons that locomotives must idle, he said.

Idling keeps the charge on the air brakes and recharges the batteries. It keeps the engine fluids from freezing on a below-freezing day.

"Sometime these engines are just hard to stop and start again" so crews keep them going, Downing said. "There's a certain amount of past practice, of course. This is just they way we've done it and the way we are always going to do it."

I found Willow Creek (the actual creek) underneath a high Hwy 96 bridge, flowing gently through tumultuous rocks, deep enough in parts to stand belly-deep in, cool and pristine. The sun is shining here, at least, glistening off the ever-wet rocks and reflecting off the water flowing down miniature Class IV rapids. A healthy array of insect life broods along the bank and the water surface and dragonflies big enough to pass for CIA drones hover synaptically around.

Willow Creek is the self-declared capital of Big Foot Country, and Sasquatch is all over, standing anywhere from 7 to 12 feet tall, altogether hairy, and weighing, I'd guess, around 500 pounds. He's pushing wheelbarrows of dirt to help the Natives' plant gardens, assisting the local settlers (obviously indifferent to invasive species) constructing the town, and even has his own museum here. Restaurants, hotels, and various other enterprises bear his namesake and use his signature footprint as imagery, and somewhere out in these temperate coastal cliffs he lurks, in packs, burying his own.

*

On a man-made dirt bluff on a steep mountainside overlooking the Trinity River, just off Hwy 299 across from some trailer park, deer rustled the leaves below, the cadence of cicadas filled the air, and I set up my tent for the night. Long after dark, while asleep, some sort of wretched wildebeest came down the stamped dirt

self-imposed campsite

path, snarling from the safety net of shadow and not so much barking as just coughing/growling intermittently, sounding too much unlike a dog, unless a very sickly one. It stayed there in the shadows, obviously bothered by my presence but not seeming too intimidated by me either. The line between the surreal and reality was thin, but I was not dreaming. In my mind it looked like one of those ravenous Worgs the Orc ride in *Lord of the Rings*. I thought it was maybe someone's guard dog, but why then did it not approach me earlier when I was setting up my tent? Perhaps *this* was Big Foot! I reached quietly for my knife and stared out of the mesh into the dark for many minutes, unconvinced that I could really do much of anything if it were something dangerous. I sat motionless, for a long time, listening to its guttural noises, until suddenly it was as if I had found the beast's eyes with my own, and the noises stopped. It disappeared, and later returned. However, by the second time, I was far too tired to care. By morning there was no trace and I packed up my things as usual. Tonight I will be comforted by the banshee-squeal of trains, and if I'm lucky, one might just side for me.

Redding, CA- 7.5 dollars to take the bus to Weaverville from Willow Creek (driver let me ride on student-fare), two hours spent at the Book Mine (nothing

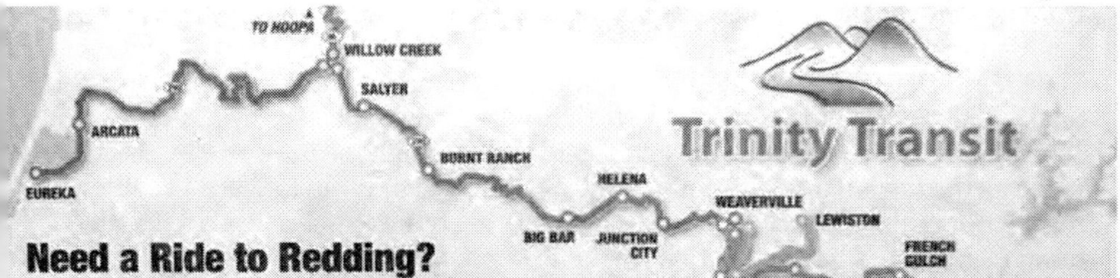

bought), and $10 for the connec bus to Redding (every scumbag a their mother tried to tell the driver they were a college student and he wasn't buying any of it). The heat here is brutal, and from it there is no respite. The downtown RABA bus depot is full of skuzzards and waistoids holding plastic bottles of sucrose and asking repetitively for cigarettes, assuming that everybody smokes. One bum relaxed in the shade in front of the closed Amtrak station, reeking from quite a distance, while another drank malt liquor on the tracks under the bridge where a perpetual -just-pissed-himself odor reigns. I know of no decent places to kill time or where even to get something to eat. The only good thing I can say of Redding is that I saw my first freight trains in over a month.

There's a layup along the mainline five or six blocks south of the downtown bus depot with a string of empty lumber cars, a woodchip car, and a couple tankers that I am electronically told were "strategically placed" there exactly this time yesterday. The other line there—about six or seven junky lumber cars—have been sitting there for a while their bad local graffiti tells me. Across from the layup is a railroad hobby shop that never seems to be open. If it had been, or if I knew of a gas station or market nearby, I may wait a day to see about catching a train out of here, but based on my past experiences in Redding, I tend to want to get in and get out as quickly as possible. The only question now is which way to go.

Shasta Lake, CA- Four buses and ten hours of travel later, I am sitting with my back against the ballast of the UP mainline as the sun sets over the Trinity Alps. (The bus runs up here from Redding—Route #1—but you have to take Route #14

Mossbrae Falls mural in Shasta Lake

from downtown and transfer at Masonic Drive. The #1 departs every hour on the hour from there and the #14 leaves every hour on the half-hour from downtown. Together they cost $2.25). With a few hours of exhaustive sunlight left I arrived in Shasta Lake, a Redding suburb that is rightfully its own modest town on the southern tip of Shasta Lake, the lake, which, confusingly, seems to go by the same name as the town. I stood thumbing the northbound onramp (a place I've hitched from before), the brutal California sun sweltering but waning. I was tired and hungry and would have liked to have made it to Dunsmuir for a fresh starting tomorrow, but eventually I resigned to camping another night and starting fresh from *here* with a cardboard sign in the morning. I walked back westward through

back on tracks- Shasta Lake, CA

town, stopped at the Sunshine Market for something to eat, and then found the tracks crossing over Shasta Blvd. There's a siding, a spur-track that breaks off and then abruptly stops, and a large gravel lot beside the tracks with a junky, overgrown loading-dock that looked suitable to camp on for the night. The sound of nearby industries churn in the air.

*

Trains blew by in the night and I awoke early this morning to a dying phone, no charger, and an urgent-sounding message from an old roommate in Portland. I just got served, she informed me. I'm being sued. Thanks.

Once again I stood on the Shasta Lake onramp with a sign and my thumb, but again resigned by the heat of day. Though it's possible, Shasta Lake is not a great spot to hitch north from (instead I'd suggest continuing south on the #1 bus and getting off at Cascade Blvd, an exit closer to town where there is a more-direct onramp that I've successfully hitched from before too), but after receiving word from my friend Aware that he might be coming through Redding to take me up on a road trip to Burney and McCloud, I regressed all the way back into town.

The heat was on again and Redding was no less frustrating, or tolerable. I saw familiar faces downtown and on the bus, and I bided my time by exploring the

trestle over the Sacramento River- Redding, CA

enormous 4,300-foot-long railroad trestle that I've ridden across numerous times, but have never stopped to admire. The trestle is 70-years old, a Warren deck truss bridge passing 110-feet above the emerald green Sacramento. It was first put into use in 1942 with the building of Shasta Dam, which effectively inundated 26 miles of existing track. That called for a realignment of the SP line which in turn necessitated eight additional bridges and twelve new tunnels through the Shasta hills. Both the construction of the higher line and the building of the Shasta Dam were important local projects at the time because they brought jobs to the region during the Great Depression. Today, the lack of camps and any sign of hobo life under or around the trestle makes me think they do nightly patrols to prevent camping. Otherwise the bridge is a decent place to catch some solitude and shade.

Eventually the day cooled as it clouded over, but not wanting to spend another minute in Redding (in case Aware got caught up and wasn't able to come through), I boarded a 19-seat bus with five other folks (not counting the driver) and took it an hour east on 299, back up a thousand feet of elevation to where it was 10-15 degrees cooler—Modoc Country—the sky above the Sierras dark and stormy and to the setting west on fire.

Burney is a high-desert logging town, like Bend, but has a downtown that is now mostly shuttered. I'm sitting on a bench in front of the Safeway, tummy full, drink on, wondering how I'm going to get to that hundred-plus-foot waterfall tomorrow.

Burney, CA- Burney Falls is a 129-foot-high cataract of frigid degree cascading forth at 3,000-feet elevation in Lassen National Forest. Hwy 89 is built almost right through the falls, and you can hear the water roar from just up the cliff. President Roosevelt, when visiting in the 1930s, called Burney Falls the Eighth Wonder of the World. But the mystery behind it is really one of geologic principal that, while fantastically unique, is repeated throughout the Shasta region. Like Mossbrae Falls north of Dunsmuir, Burney Falls is spring-fed. Five underground aquifers seep through thousands of rivulets across a porous basalt cliff face, the result of a 1.8-million-year-old lava flow that covered the valley. But unlike Mossbrae Falls, Burney Falls is also fed by a creek that drains the runoff and glacial melt from Burney Mountain. Burney Falls is a sort of wide, double-decker waterfall that is gargantuan; to truly get a feel for the sheer power behind its beauty try standing on the nearest unsubmerged rock in front of its roaring face. As it spits frigidly at you in rainbows everything just becomes silver looking in the mist.

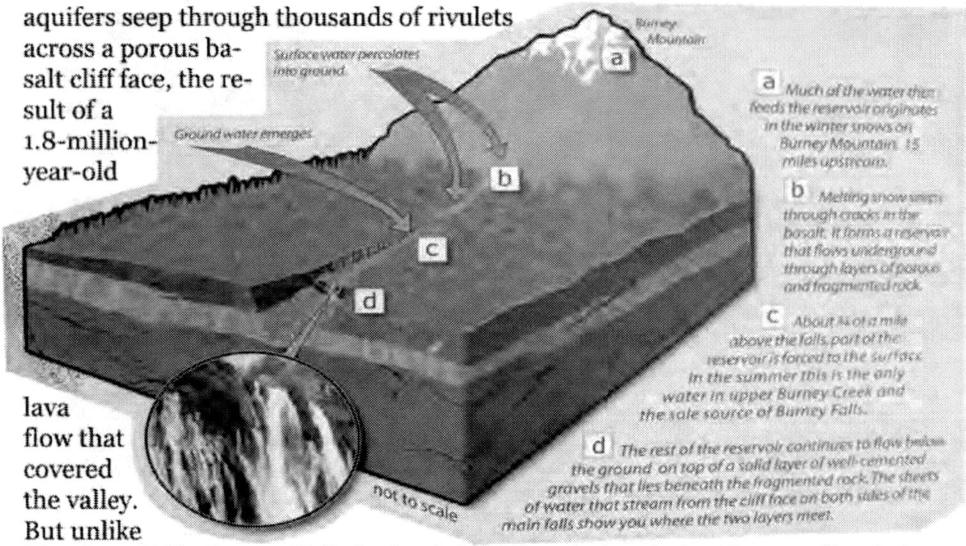

The native inhabitants of the Burney Falls area were the Pit River[28] People, named because of a hunting technique they employed to catch large game by trapping them in deep pits. But in spite of the Natives, Burney Falls received the name of a drifter from South Carolina.

---

28. flows from high up in Modoc National Forest, southwest into Shasta Lake, and like Shasta Lake, the Pit River has Lake Britton, a dam-created reservoir just north of Burney.

Burney Falls

Samuel Burney was caretaking the farm of a well-to-do man named Thomas Preadmore, who had angered the Natives by mistreating Indian women, apparently. Burney ultimately paid the price for Preadmore's crimes when vengeance struck in the name of the Indian Warrior, and as a result, the falls, the mountain, the creek, and the town, are memorialized in his name.

Today, Burney Falls is as it was long before it took its current name, but ever so subtly it is changing, constantly. Erosion is actually causing the falls to slowly retreat upstream about a tenth of an inch a year. But you'd be hard-pressed to notice much change beyond the foliage. There's a hiking trail that circles the falls and from which you can walk atop it, but every local we spoke to seemed to have a story about someone who died trying to jump from there. Looking out over its pouring ledge you can see that there are massive outcroppings to clear, and though I'm sure there's a significantly deep plunge pool below, I never got the panicky feeling that I was seriously going to attempt that jump. Perhaps in the future.

*

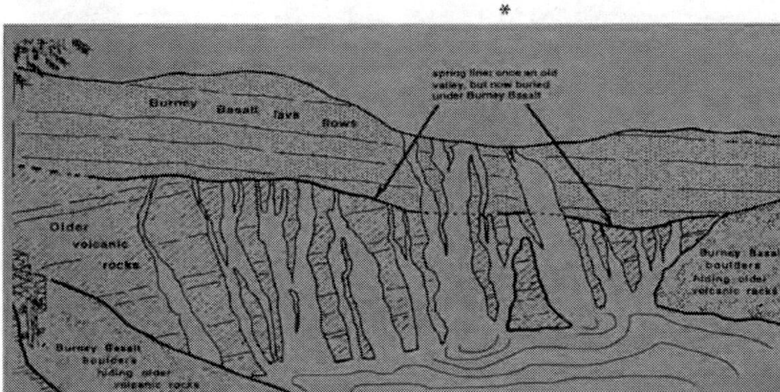

One to two million years ago, the Burney Basalt lavas erupted and partially filled an older valley in this area. In the current face of the Falls, water seeping through the Burney Basalt lavas — but *not* the older rocks the lavas covered — emerges as springs at the base of the Burney Basalt. The rocks beneath the spring line are largely impermeable volcanic mudflows and sediments 10 to 25 million years old.

Trains no longer run to Burney. The McCloud River Railroad dwindled in its final decade until the shortline hauled one final load back across the Lake Britton Bridge in 2006 (nascent train-riding years for me). But it is because of the now-abandoned train bridge over this manmade reservoir that the McCloud River Railroad will for long be steeped in American popular culture.

Built in 1954 for the short-lived extension to Burney, the train bridge operated well into the new millennia, seeing its last train across as recently as July 1, 2006. But the most important role of the bridge by far was its cameo appearance in the 1986 classic *Stand By Me*, a film about four small-town friends who set out to find a dead body that is rumored to be lying somewhere along the rails. While filmed largely in Oregon (in the towns of Brownsville, Eugene, and Cottage Grove), arguably the most memorable scene from the film takes place here at Lake Britton in California. Up until now I thought the location of the bridge was somewheres on the Siskiyou Line in Southern Oregon, perhaps crossing the Umpqua or Rogue River, and did not know until recently that the scene was filmed here. But one look at the curving, fir-draped canyon wall and I had no doubt that I was looking south across the same high trestle where Vern and Gordy ran from an momentous 72-ton McCloud River Railroad steam engine, nearly perishing, both, in the film. But while there is a paralleling Hwy-89-that lends support for the panoramic camera shots in the film, you wouldn't necessarily know from the Hwy that this is The Bridge; you've got to walk up to its edge. (The Bridge also appeared in a 1994 music video for Aerosmith's *Livin' On The Edge*.)

Stand By Me

I can only imagine the bridge in its heyday, when tramps were lucky enough to ride across on freight trains and tramp freely around the eastern flank of Shasta. The steel rails have now been torn up and sold for scrap, the bridge barbwire-fenced off and blocked by concrete barricades, but that didn't stop us from climbing out, around on, and eventually even jumping off it into the lake (though not from all the way up on the tracks, I admit, but from a crossbeam 15-or-so-feet lower (see inside back cover). However, shimmying across the underbelly of the bridge out onto that beam high above the concrete foundation was just as imper-

Lake Britton Bridge

iling I'm sure. And it was still a 75 - 80-foot jump that caused the Chinese family fishing on the shore to gawk).

The McCloud River Railroad came into existence in 1897 first and foremost as a logging railroad. The extension to Burney was added in 1955 when the McCloud River Lumber Company purchased the harvesting rights to 80,000 acres of pine forest south of Burney. The lumber company then financed the railroads extension, saying there was enough timber to keep trains running for fifty years. They ran for fifty-one. The railroad continued to operate well through the 1990s benefiting from its placement between two major rail lines—the SP (now UP) to the west and BN (now BNSF) east—and accessing each through opposite junctions-Mt. Shasta on the SP and Lookout Junction on the BN. But after the inevitable implosion of local timber and the consolidation of the railroad industry itself, only one or two industries remained to be served and the cost for maintaining the rails became too much. The Lookout Line was last used December 2003, and shortly after, its trackage ripped up. For a few more years the railroad continued to hang on, mostly by dabbling in tourism with a local Dinner Train that ran from Mt. Shasta. But in October 2006, shortly after it's last run to Burney, the McCloud River Railroad abandoned all its trackage

ex-track bed

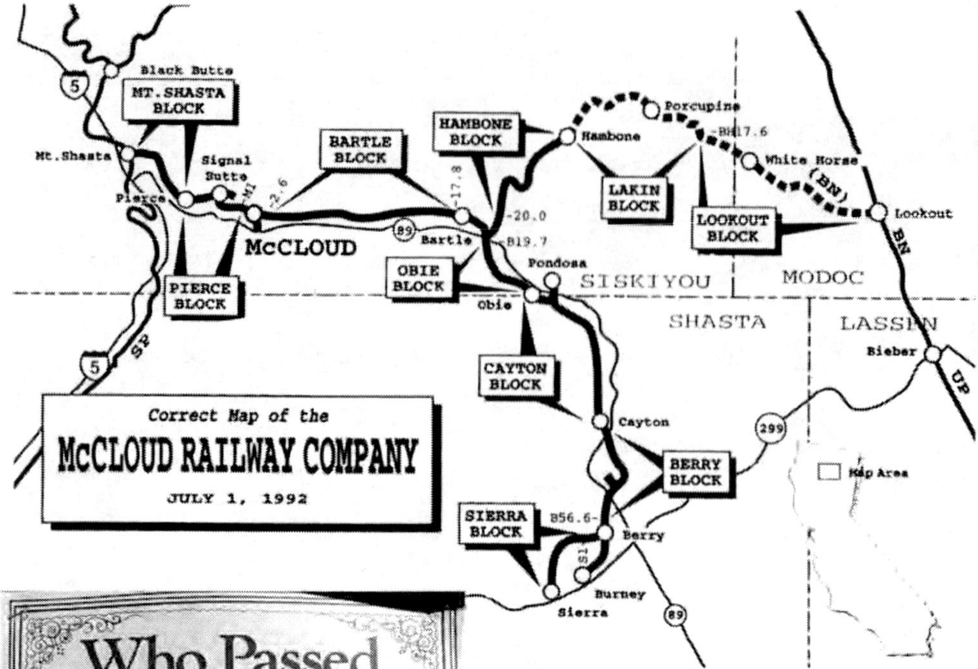

east of McCloud, the yard almost overnight becoming shuttered.

Except for on the Lake Britton Bridge where thick creosote ties are still in place to walk across, the tracks are entirely removed from Burney until around Bartle, fifteen miles east of McCloud. Hwy 89, which largely parallels the old train route, intersects the railroad grade not far from Burney. The crossing is now exempt, and burgundy-red ballast heads straight off at a forty-five-degree angle to the Hwy in both directions and is now an in-the-works hiking trail linking Burney to McCloud. However, usership is currently at an all-time low, and so in a big silver pickup truck we drove off onto the railroad grade and followed the track's original route—the closest you can come to riding this line today.

Kicking up a red dust, we came to the remnants of an old watertank once used to fill steam engines. The base structure was still intact but the actual watertank had been decimated and reduced to a hanging spigot and some stray metal rebar. Further along, just past a dirt road crossing, we came to an old wooden, trackside shack that looked untouched since its abandonment.

McCloud, CA- One Ross McCloud settled here in 1855 but the McCloud River took its name twenty-five years earlier from a Hudson Bay Trapper named Alexander McLeod. Various spellings were used alternately throughout the early years, but today the latter reigns.

Back in its heyday there could not have been a more beautiful or peaceful place to work, as far as railroading goes. The old McCloud yard sprawls for acres under the looming presence of Mt. Shasta, winding back on red-rock ballast through Douglas fir and ponderosa pines, crossing over pristine flowing creeks. With the short jaunt from Mt. Shasta to McCloud still functional, the yard today is mainly used to store empty lumber racks, yet remains old-fashioned and largely undismantled. Within it are old wooden structures, watertanks, ancient passenger trains and cabooses, and several sawed-off McCloud River Railroad boxcars with the railroad's logo rusting away prominently on display. That logo, an image of a bear balancing on a log with a fish in its mouth and a profile of Mt. Shasta in the background (or just a bear with a fish in its mouth in front of a generic mountain), was the result of a local school contest and to this day remains a classic image in western railroading, exemplifying perfectly the raw beauty imbedded in the frontier-west and the railroad's ties to nature through industry.

Walking through the yard, I felt like I was exploring a ghost town. There showed evidence of people, of workers, but I saw no one. Roads were visibly worn down yet overgrown, buildings were still full of old equipment, and all around the yard things were left eerily intact, like one day everyone just suddenly stopped working, but were expecting to return. Looking inside the scale house, for example, I saw through the window a pencil lying on a sheet of paper that it had marked, while a lone sweatshirt remained hanging on a hook against the back wall. After dark, lights glowed from within one of the office buildings where company awards and framed engine-pictures still hang in the

McCloud River Railroad yard- McCloud, CA

Hwy 299, Northern California. December 2011

Cascade Mountains, Oregon. January 2012

having only done once before I'm not as familiar with), a northbound BNSF passed on the adjacent track just as the DPU I was in ended its forty-five minutes of idleness and began to move south. In an instant I jumped off to catch north the line of all empty well-cars instead. But I hesitated on that too. It was eveningtime already and I didn't know if I wanted to ride north then or camp out again and wait until morning. But the train stopped right in front of me and did not air up again until I found an empty 48" to ride; and since I know that the subdivision to Bend is extremely rural and not one where riding an empty well-car would be considered dangerous, I hopped on, glad to be on the move again.

Passing back by the southbound catch-out spot where the night before I had waited, I looked out and saw Forrest lying on a splayed cardboard-box reading the zine I gave to him. Rachel was beside him, on her stomach, sleeping, and I hollered and waved.

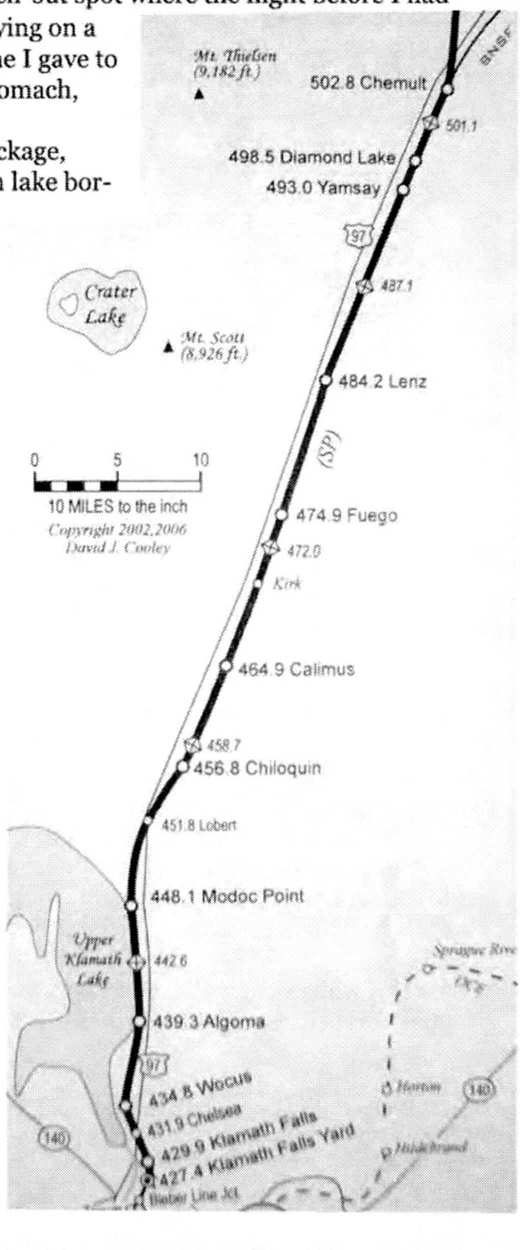

Rolling north on UP/BNSF joint trackage, along the east bank of a true mountain lake bordered by uplifted ridges on both sides—the largest fresh body of water in Oregon—I stood in the front of the well-car so that in case a passing southbound came I could get down out of its view—the only visibility issue I was worried about. It's pretty much a straight shot, four hours rushing through the high-desert forest to Bend, and BNSF runs it hard, even with junk. The only time the train slowed was at Chemult, where UP's tracks divaricate northwest into the Cascades on the Natron Cutoff (BNSF keeps a NNE trajectory).

Chemult[12], a tiny town located near Crater Lake that was formed by the railroad in 1926, is the closest Amtrak station to Bend, and a rural outpost at that. Dozens of passengers stood on the *new* Amtrak station platform waiting for the probably-late Coast Starlight to wisk them off south, and I wondered what they'd say if they saw me cheating the system like I was.

As the sun lowered behind a thin wall of not-tall ponderosas and the wind grew colder, I sat on my pack.

12. named after a Klamath Indian Chief.

tion that has taken over in the past few years—an excruciating amount. It's pretty, Bend is, with the Cascades in close range still capped with snow, the river running through and the fresh mountain air. But it's all too nice you soon realize—too perfect. There is money in Bend, not necessarily to be made, but to be spent, and the rapid influx of people over the past decade consists mainly of middle and upper class retirees and young urban professionals. It's a similar trend happening elsewhere in the state, most noticeably in Portland, where using the prefix "eco" or anything "organic" is bound to strike gold with the yuppies and hipsters. Bend's worse though. Here, there's little if any counter-culture to counter the gentrification that is like a runaway greenhouse effect.

You know that one REI-guru with shaggy blonde hair and perpetually tanned skin who wears only alternative brand-name clothing, khaki shorts, and leather sandals, that outdoorsy, rock-climbing backpacker type who can afford to do every Winter Olympic sport year-round with the most up-to-date gear? I saw him walking up to the REI scratch-and-dent sale this morning alongside a girl ten years his younger who could be a model for (the hideous) Wend Magazine. Once I saw that guy bro-in' across the street like a burnt-out old surfer that owns the town, I knew just what kind of place Bend has become to attract these types of people.

I was in the wretched Old Mill District, which very recently popped up from its industrial ashes to brood yuppies and retirees like a cruise ship. It's an inner-city suburb of high-end recreational retail stores, "boutiques," "organic cafes," and riverside "bistros" to the extent that it sickens me. Two blocks in I stopped a woman walking her too-coddled dog to ask her, very seriously, *How* do I get out of here? She looked at my haggard profile and laughed, then pointed me in the direction of downtown. It was about a mile of a walk along Riverside through upscale residential neighborhoods, and all the while I was thinking, *If Forrest and Rachel grew up here, where the fuck are they from?*

*

Yesterday, while sitting aboard a southbound BNSF in Klamath Falls, unsure if I wanted to yet ride south and if I was prepared to take the BNSF route[11] (which

11. which follows the Modoc Northern line SE of Klamath Falls to Merrill, OR before breaking E to Malin, OR, and from there turning S into the Modoc National Forest of Northern California and continuing S through Lookout and Bieber, following the Pit River briefly, then winding S to Keddie Junction and linking up with UP's Feather River trackage.

and through my head's thin hair . . . barreling through the Antelope Desert at Fuego—mile 479.7—a straightaway of track with a tree line to the east . . . the mountains suddenly disappearing and the land looking like it's been glacier-flattened to a pasture, across miles and miles of which are further-distant mountains . . . straightaway through Lenz: Klamath Wildlife Refuge east and Crater Lake National Park due west . . . a gutted metal building with a lonely loading dock—once a factory of some sort . . . the tracks curving slightly east, then keeping straight . . . Yamsay—mile 492—no cars and nothing sided . . . passing Diamond Lake . . . hills returning and the train beginning to take more curves . . . slowing on the mainline . . . pulling onto Chemult, a curved siding of sloped, sand-colored rock . . . veering northeast at the junction where UP and BNSF tracks diverge . . . people waiting at the Amtrak station for a train . . . blowing through Rosedale with no stopping . . . into the high desolate desert of Deschutes National Forest . . . nothingness . . . Wickiup Jct . . . Rosland Road . . . Newberry Crater National Monument . . . Wickiup Reservation . . . the town I'm passing through now—I'm not sure—but I just stood up and looked right at a cop car sitting on the side of the Hwy facing me . . . suddenly in the middle of the Newberry National Volcanic Monument, one of the most otherworldly sects of track I've ever ridden through, a veritable lava field spread over hundreds of acres of forestland . . . the train creeping through craggy basalt rock on fairly level track with not a tall tree in sight and visibility opening up for miles in all directions . . . now barreling into Bend, and it should be a pretty quick CC so I'm going to have to have my stuff together . . .

northbound to Bend

Bend, OR- Bend got its name from a double-bend section of the Deschutes River that earned the name Farewell Bend because it was for early emigrants their last sight of the river after crossing westward. This wasn't the only Farewell Bend in Oregon[10], but it was a relatively easy place to ford the not-so-subtle Deschutes and a place where travelers "fared well" before moving on. Some never left. The railroad reached in Bend in 1911 with the Great Northern Railway elbowing its way down the Deschutes River from the Columbia, and a line connecting to SP's Natron Cutoff to California (the line I just rode up from Klamath Falls) opened in 1928 with all eyes on profiting from the surrounding timber.

Today, Bend might as well be called Gend due to the unprecedented gentrifica-

10. The original Oregon Trail passed through an area on the Snake River border of Oregon and Idaho known to travelers as Farewell Bend that today retains that name as a memorial park.

ride south with two DPUs directly under the bridge. I might as well take it, I thought. The Daily 203 Card had been inspected two days prior in Vancouver, the day before in Pasco, and not yet today, so that was to be expected. I sat aboard the BNSF DPU idling on the tracks of UP's yard in Klamath Falls.

*

Upper Klamath Lake marshland

Upper Klamath Lake: lush, green, full, and refreshing looking . . . (I want this train to stop so I can swim in it) . . . the Hwy mirroring the tracks then disappearing . . . the tracks following a stream that diverts from the Lake: the Williamson River, a marvelous little stream in a very picturesque watershed . . . two kids swimming in the river, and I looking down at them and waving, but they don't see me or pay notice to the train passing above them . . . in Chiloquin a five-story grain mill looking like a big building all by itself . . . but it's nothing . . . gaining elevation . . . looking over ponderosa pines, sagebrush desert, and birch trees to the Klamath Mountains far west . . . the tracks winding through a high rolling desert, cutting through the hills as the train stays level along what looks like a dry riverbed that's filled with stout trees and shrubs . . . the smell of burnt rubber . . . screeching along curving tracks . . . dirt country roads . . . not a car in sight and there hasn't been for miles . . . mile 463.8 . . . Where am I *on the back of a stop sign at Calimus . . . Winema National Forest . . . the rocky Williamson River gulch to the west where the river flowing through is miniscule, yet used to be canyonesque . . . the train clearly climbing in elevation . . . steep red rocks east . . . vultures hovering—turkey vultures . . . the stream, essentially a coulee . . . a waxing half-moon rising to the southeast, directly behind me, and the gulch getting deeper and gulchier . . . green light ahead . . . train leveling out a bit and picking up speed . . . mile 468.2 . . . two large Cascadian peaks visible ahead . . . sun sinking low in the western sky, just above the tops of trees . . . and soon an area where there's obviously been some burn and the trees are scarcer . . . crossing a river, the Williamson still . . . another dirt road-crossing and still not a car in sight . . . through an area of burned and chopped-down trees . . . the warm wind blowing on my face*

Williamson River

Klamath Falls- One good thing about adhering to the crust-punk dress code is you'll find almost instant camaraderie wherever you go. A downside would be the profiling. But Forrest and Rachel, brother and sister traveling together from Bend, said it rarely happens to them and have received no such profiling in Klamath Falls. Instead they found kind of a punk-squat in a four-story Elks Lodge downtown (which sounded to me quite righteous). Every little town we talked about—Bend, Petaluma, Monterey, etc.—they made sound like each had a brotherhood of crusties to get put up with, not to mention the more major hubs like Eugene, Portland, and Seattle. It's like you sew on some GBH patch, wear all black, get a couple of bad tattoos, and all the time get "shit-faced" on cheap beer and you've got a brotherhood wherever you end up—Crust-punks, the new generation of rail tramps, replacing the FTRA-era rabble-rousers and pathologically-lying "Vietnam Vets."

I watched the sun set on the tracks in K-Falls talking to Forrest—a big kid who's only been riding about a year, and who tends to live between Eugene, Portland, and his hometown Bend—and his sister Rachel—a tattoo artist from Bend who wore a colorful array of them on her chest, as well as a skillfully patched miniskirt and 60s horn-rimmed glasses. Rachel has bleached blonde hair. Forrest's head is shaved. I thought about how, as Rachel sewed the front of an old, black-and-white Ice-Cube t-shirt onto a butt flap, about how well they'd fit into the crust-drunk scene I stumbled on in Spokane at the Checkerboard Tavern[9], and how very similar—almost identical—her and Forrest were to a couple of tattooed punks that worked there. We sat behind an abandoned building at the north end of the yard, drank beers, and shot the shit as they waited for a UP train south.

Ice-Cube and Rachel

At least two southbound UPs came through in the night, as well as one piggyback (an intermodal-carrying train) this morning, all of which stopped directly on the mainline to crew-change (CC) but none of which Forrest and Rachel managed to catch. Two mornings in a row a UP train CCed just before sunrise as BNSF waited for clearance northbound, which then departed at a catchable speed of 6–8 mph—both mornings. Two other southbound UPs later came though, and around 1600, as I was back down under the Sixth St. Bridge looking to catch-out, a southbound BNSF came through and stopped, presenting itself as a legitimate

9. see: *Railroad Semantics #5*

Klamath Falls, OR Aug. 2011

Klamath Falls, OR Aug. 2011

Earth Quake 11-26-91
John EASLEY 84
Earth Quake 9-14-92
Hot Shot
Pocatello Paul 6-26-93
his NAME IS WARREN FROM TEXAS — WATCH 'EM
CAPT. HOOK
Chilly in K. FALLS
Shoestring
BAD KS ROUNDS COMIN
THE TEXAS MAD MAN 6-19-93
SOME ARE SATISFIED TO SIT BY THE SIDE & WATCH THE TRAINS ROLL BY
THAT AINT ME TOO MUCH TO SEE
GONNA ROLL TILL I DIE
NORTH BANK FRED 10-93
GRANDPA OTTRA 4-16-94
Big-BubbA 6-2-93 Crazy Train

Klamath Falls, OR Aug. 2011

Klamath Falls, OR

G.S.
6-11 COALTRAIN
RYE
10
WHISTLEPIG
STRAIGHT RYE
WHISKEY
Bigfoot
Rafting
PALE ALE
HUMBOLDT
WILDLIFE
CARE CENTER
WTF

Conductor takes a smoke break

to the river's west bank. This rhythm is repeated over and over between Castle Crag and O'Brien—a distance of about forty-miles—as the train passes back and forth underneath the sharp curving, diverging I-5 Interstate, which manages to avoid all tunnels by skimming along the tops of the Shasta hills, though not without suffering much more drastic 'clines.

Shasta Lake crevice

The Sacramento feeds directly into the red, striated, splayed-arm crevices of Shasta Lake, a manmade reservoir that feeds Southern California a lot of water. Peter Skene Ogden first recorded the name Sastise, as the Native Americans throughout the region were known, in his journal back in 1827, then naming the Mountain[35]. The word today denotes a mountain, a river, a valley, a town, a lake, a dam, a forest, and a county. The dam, a towering concrete wall six-hundred-feet high, located just below the confluence of the Sacramento and Pit rivers, was constructed over a seven-year period beginning in 1937 and created Shasta Lake by damming the flows of several creeks and rivers, including the Pit, Sacramento, and McCloud. Twenty-six miles of SP track then had to be raised and realigned, causing a network of small copper-mining communities linked by rail to be abandoned. Kennett was the largest, once holding a population of over 5,000. But Kennett, like the other towns, went under during the Great Depression as the copper mining industry faltered; and then with completion of the dam, literally went under. Kennet was the first to be flooded as the backed-up-river-waters rose, and legend has it that the Lake filled much quicker than expected and the town was not able to be fully dismantled, only cleared out, and that during a drought, when the water is low, you can see the top of a steeple from one of the old churches poking out above the water down by the dam. Now, whenever crossing Shasta Lake, I think about all the underwater towns be-

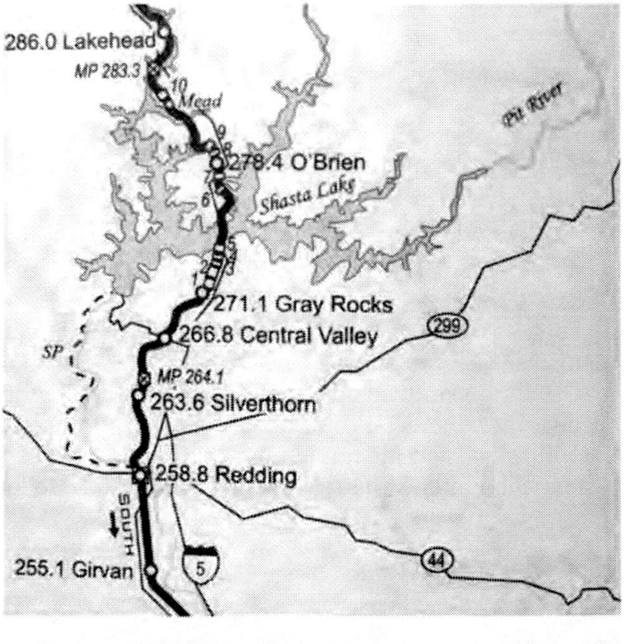

35. that the Natives called Wy-e-kah.

neath, along with the network of underground railroad tunnels burrowing through the hills like sea caves.

The tracks cross sections of the Lake's arms on impressive trestles, and the heartiest portion on the Pit River Bridge, a colossal, single-track, double-decker, dual road and rail cantilever bridge of full force. Built in 1942 during the construction of Shasta Dam, the Pit River Bridge is the highest rail bridge ever built in the U.S.- five-hundred-feet high from the original level of the river[36]. The bridge spans 2,754-feet long[37], and as I stood looking off the back of the unit over what *was* the Pit River Valley, I felt unparalleled and secluded viewing it as I was.

historical photo of the bridge prior to Shaska Lake

Tunnel #5 directly follows the bridge and engulfs the train. Four more tunnels are then passed through before reaching Gray Rocks, making a total of fifteen tunnels between there and Dunsmuir—a distance of just fifty-one miles, to give you an idea of how dynamic it is.

crossing the Pit River Bridge

The train stopped on the mainline north of Redding between Central Valley and Silverthorn, and T-Box and I got out and stretched our legs on the littered, red, California trackside for an hour of sunshine. When the train moved on I saw that a northbound GM had pulled onto Silverthorn to let my train pass, affirming

36. The height from rail deck to water is, of course, much less now that the Lake has been made.
37. ...on the rails. The upper roadway stretches 3,588 feet long.

what had been holding us up. We rolled steadily through Shasta Lake, the town, and I knew we were close to Redding. Paying more attention this time, I realized that no tunnel directly precedes the enormous railroad trestle crossing the Sacramento River to Redding. The train just rolls right out onto that long, eastward-curving bridge with no forewarning, the river valley wide and gorgeous, and the trestle a daunting height above the river.

I did not miss seeing Redding pass by. I could really care less about this place and it felt great to be aboard that train blowing through, leaving behind all the

crossng the trestle into Redding

cops and waistoids, that pitiless layup, the smell of perpetual piss . . . *some old, abandoned, restored passenger-cars off to the left in some field . . . an old mill and a mobile park . . . Happy Valley Rd . . . paralleling Hwy 273 . . . the Midway Market across a four-lane hwy with u-turn spots occasionally cutting through . . . 39 mph . . . Medina's Custom Cabinets . . . small antique shops . . . a crossing where there's a gravel truck waiting . . . a cluster of four palm trees—three of them in a row . . . gravel industry and a spur track leading back . . . a railroad signal passing at eye level . . . 31 mph; fuel at 3,010 gallons . . . Siskiyou Forest Products . . . Vaughn's market—abandoned . . . Sierra Pacific Windows with a very M.C. Escheresque logo . . . another used car lot with little flags hanging parabolically . . . a spur track leading back to lumber industry . . . Sprinkles Rd: cars lined up waiting for the train to pass . . . (I feel like I could go to sleep) . . . slowing . . . 15 mph . . . through a small Gervais-like* (Gervais, Oregon) *town . . . track work ahead (is why the train is going so slow)—I'm crouching down to hide so the workers don't see my silhouette . . . now back up to 15 mph . . . Hwy 273 crossing over the tracks . . . the Valley very flat and the train picking up speed to 32 . . . trains laid-up and loaded with lumber in front of a largely abandoned lumber mill . . . (T-Box is sunk down in the Conductor's chair) . . . a three-way-stop road-crossing . . . fields of tall grass and cattle fences but no cattle . . . (I could go to sleep any time) . . . an abandoned spur track trailing northwestward back to some abandoned industry . . . 40 mph, but not seeming like we're going that fast at all; fuel down to 3000 . . . the word Phoenix on an old building . . . train curving west . . . prairies, pastures, and farmland stretch east to the Sierra Nevadas . . . a moat/swamp off to the right, short birch and drought-tolerant trees of all kinds . . . train screeching, arching westward . . . white pickup truck stopped on the side of the road and a women getting out and walking over to her mailbox . . . a worker-truck hiding in the bushes (the workers are sneaky, and they're all out working on stuff today 'cause it's nice out) . . . a pasture with horses and then a pasture with sheep, followed by a larger pasture with cattle . . . three big telephone line/internet towers in a row . . . more pastures . . . an empty, damaged jukebox on the side of the tracks . . . another small town that I can't see the name of—something with a C . . . the roadway canalling under the tracks and Hwy 273 crossing over . . . litter under the bridge and buff marks . . . a small, shallow river that could be the Sacramento, but it's much slower moving now . . . hay meadows cut and plowed geometrically to my left, another gravel lot to the right . . . a big double-length gravel-carrying semi-truck at the crossing . . . a house with a nice yard and a bunch of abandoned stuff and cows that look obese—it's nice property with old-fashioned tractors and the cattle just lazing in the grass not at all startled by the train . . . now moving at 41 mph, and seeming to go that fast; 2,990 gallons of fuel . . . a road crossing with cars backed way back . . . a house built on stilts sits on the ground to the left . . . pastures on both sides of the train . . . Draper: nothing sided . . . an emaciated, decomposing cattle carcass within the boundary of the cattle fence, just lying there decomposing . . . hills that look like an old battlefield the way the rocks are strategically placed like defensive forts . . . abandoned cars . . . Hooker Creek and McCoy Rd . . . a jeep with two bikes on the back, drives north on McCoy Road . . . the tracks now elevating on a hill . . . 31 mph; fuel 2980 . . . mile 283.7 . . . on the downslope doing an easy 38—now 40 miles per hour . . . dried out channelbeds . . . the tracks sort of elevated on a hill with the land more rolling now, a mixture of short green and tall bleached-grass . . . somebody's illegally-dumped pile of baby toys . . . two lines of stone statue-things lead to a driveway back to some estate . . . cactus with little red buckeye things on the tops of them grow in the channelbeds in short clumps . . . Blunt. The name of the siding is Blunt . . . coasting at 45 mph; fuel at 2970 . . . a third track on the siding appearing in very obvious abandon . . . Train slowing to about 34 . . . 32 mph . . . now really lunging . . .*

Twenty miles of small trackside towns and the train came to Red Bluff. I immediately recognized it but couldn't keep conscious past the sleep I did not get. I dozed off on the floor of the unit for twenty-or-so-minutes, and before I knew it the train was approaching Chico . . . *nearing the heart of the Central Valley . . . a huge industrial green house with thick white plastic and a pointy top . . . fields so freshly tilled they glisten . . . piles of burning yard debris . . . almond orchards . . . 48 mp, window slightly ajar . . . equines grazing, solar panels on a rooftop, an old shack . . . 187.5 mile marker on the back of a corrugated-metal building . . . storage units . . . 1950s automobiles—abandoned . . . a bright yellow container with a hose . . . about twenty cars waiting at a four-lane crossing . . . train bumping up and down . . . 48 miles per hour . . . Another two-lane crossing . . . a big, three-story red barn and a graffitied wall . . . a red sleeping bag out in the orchard where someone's been sleeping under one of the trees . . . eight or nine cars at a two-lane road crossing . . . Gomes on the back of a wooden fence . . . more storage units . . . a trailer park . . . an athletic field . . . The Oasis . . . (I'm looking for Sierra Nevada, my back stiff in the chair as we pass through the*

Chico yard

almond orchard

crossing) . . . yellow water tower . . . Chico California Amtrak station . . . [crossing bell dings audibly] . . . *18 mph . . . CP VP 184 Chico . . . train slowing considerably . . . a really nice, expansive backyard garden in a triangular shape with a scarecrow . . . train slowing to 10 mph . . . a row of old logs . . . really, really bad graffiti on a big brown wall—really bad! . . . 5.9 . . .* [engine hisses] . . . *5.4 . . .* [sounds of air being viciously cut] *(Did you hear that? What the fuck was that?) . . .*

The train stopped in Chico's yard and we got off. The mainline was unobstructed to my right, and on the left sat a line of hoppers in the yard—always hoppers in Chico. On the other side of the mainline was a almond-tree orchard with a thick growth of really green, parsley-looking grass on the ground between rows. A southbound hotshot soon passed on the mainline, one that if we would have waited at Maxwell last night we would have probably caught around midnight or 1, but would have then had to suffer on overnight through the frigid Cascade Mountains. I'm glad we didn't and instead rode in style.

Standing in the orchard, a worker's legs suddenly appeared, walking lazily on the opposite side of the train. I grew tense as he approached the DPU, and, crouching in the orchard, got ready to meet him at its door when he climbed on. But he never did. He simply rounded the back end of the DPU, walked back up along the other side of the train, and continued up the rest of the line on the orchard side. I deduced it was the Engineer taking a stroll, killing time till clearance came; and about the time he would have made it back up to the engine—an amount of time equal to when the train first stopped to when I saw his feet appear—the DPU hissed air and began to inch onward south.

Sacramento Valley

It was an inconsistent rest of the ride through a very consistent landscape of flat, endlessly arable farm plots and orchards, with a two-lane road running alongside the tracks, and small town after small town being passed through . . . *lots of trash dumped along the tracks—couches, TVs—and lots of hoppers laid up in Chico . . . southbound along tilled dirt . . . Midway . . . endless acres of orchards . . . an old two-lane blacktop road . . . a viaduct over a river . . . slowing back to 18 mph; 2900 on the fuel gage . . . fields left fallow . . . moving past rice paddies . . . 29 mph; 2890 fuel . . . flat and hot in the valley . . . northbound Z-train sided at 3:17 P.M. at Richvale . . . 22 mph . . . 23 and 24 . . . (the train has been manic, going from 50 down to 14, the unit jerking all around) . . . past Biggs, going through more orchards . . . 48 mph again . . . watershed and hay fields . . . looking out the rearview mirror from the Engineer's seat at a straightway of track and a silo of some sort . . . (I've got a little bit of a headache, I think from not having any coffee) . . . a suburban neighborhood on the edge of the desert that is like an area south of Fresno where I once sided . . . lots of junk dumped along the tracks . . . Gridley, a little western town with silos and corrugated-metal buildings and the train cuts straight through everything, even the downtown . . . an abandoned warehouse with tracks not being used . . . back out into fields of grass—pastures and hay fields . . . some mountains appearing on the southwest horizon . . . 157.1 . . . red Light as the DPU passes through . . . a junkyard to the left of the train . . . orchards spanning endlessly to the horizon of very distant, craggy mountains with clouds hanging heavy above them . . . a swamp of some sort . . . Fagan siding . . . Luther . . . train at 50 mph. 2870 gallons of fuel . . . (fifty miles to Roseville) . . . a beautiful little orchard at the siding's end . . . (I wish I could have a house with Conan, Miette, and chickens, and live there with my girl, and maybe a turtle) . . . Sutter County . . . the Mendocino Mountains directly east of Williams, leading to Ukiah . . . mile 152.1 . . . finally a tree line to obscure the tracks—but it ends . . . the tracks paralleling the street to the first crossing where just one truck sits . . . the town of Sunset . . . Rudy's Auto Repair, some dental care place, Pit Bull Gym, liquor store, Tower Market, Broadway Street Lounge, Benita La Gloria . . . palm trees . . . very young trees planted in an orchard that's almost like a cemetery with the way the trees have something white wrapped around their trunks . . . 150.7 . . . a field not being used for anything but that looks great to walk with bare feet on . . . Sunset Holding Company . . . Meso, Gomes . . . a funeral-pyre-old-tower thing . . . cracked up PVC pipe piled in the corner of a field . . . just a flataway expanse . . . (this lifestyle, why would anyone give it up? It's exhaustive, that's why. Every year after another year of this I think I'll just settle down with a straight job for a little while, have my cats and have some chickens, love my girl and live it easy) . . . Live Oak Blvd, cars backed up a good fifty or sixty deep waiting for the train to pass, the Mendocino Mountains behind and huge, and a glowing gathering of cumulous hangs over the Sierra Nevadas east . . . Your Ad Here . . . fairly level track—about 0.1-percent of an incline . . . an archway*

crossing the American River

of a sort where the siding ends, Hwy off to the right, train slowing to 16 mph . . . creeping along . . . a subdivision adjacent—houses cheaply constructed, all packed in as many as can fit . . . now rising above the orchards, the air smelling of chicken compost . . . (there's someone in a boat on the river . . . I've gotta wave to them) . . . crossing the American River—maybe the Sacramento . . . rolling slow now—14; 2800 on the fuel gauge . . . it looks like the train got longer, maybe in K-Falls this morning . . . curving significantly around the fields on a kind of elevated track looking overtop the trees . . . another bridge up ahead that's trestle-like . . .

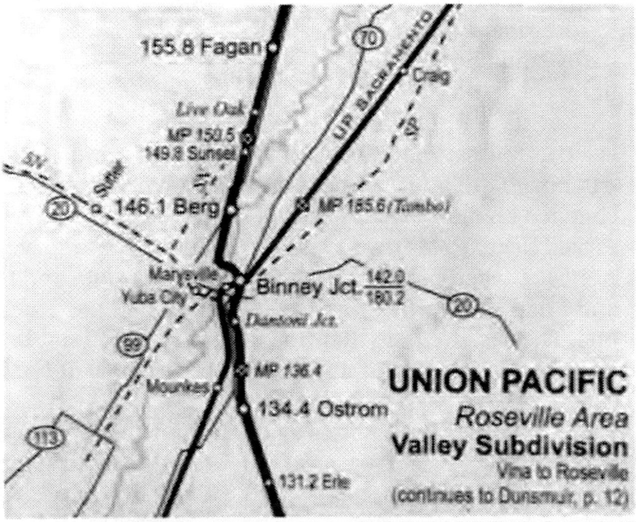

At Binney Junction in Marysville the tracks split southwest to Sacramento and southeast to Roseville, and a separate UP sub criss-crosses perpendicularly the Valley sub NE to Keddie Junction on the Feather River Route. Marysville, named in honor of Mary Murphy Covillaud, a survivor of the Donner Party, is bisected by the Feather and American Rivers and is unique in the way the tracks roll elevated above town on a flood-wall-like hill; hills surround all the rivers like levies. The train rolled elevated through town and then veered southeast to Roseville, and there were no trains at Binney Jct.'s wye of fresh ballast and newly replaced ties of the concrete variety.

Binney Junction

rolled slowly into Roseville a few hours late but otherwise as expected. While pulling in I reported from my side of the DPU that a man in a big red pickup truck was watching the DPU rather intensively from a nondescript storage unit lot. I wasn't thinking...

"I guess this guy just *really* likes to watch trains," I said, ducking down out of the way.

It took T-Box a second to respond to me: "That's Tone!"

We ran out onto the catwalk and waved enthusiastically like we were stranded, then climbed off the front of the unit while it was still rolling and Tone met us back down the tracks. It was a warm and sunny day, and I still had a bit of a headache.

Sacramento, CA- Like so many other place names in California, Sacramento's is of Spanish origin and steeped in religious connotation. The name means: The Holy. But the city, essentially named for the *river* Sacramento, really could not be any *less* holy.

After squatting in an electricity-less, water-less home with T-Box and Tone for several days, I took the #15 bus to 4th and J Street downtown, walked to the Amtrak Station, and exchanged an old Portland-to-Seattle ticket (worth fifty-two dollars) for an unreserved ticket to Martinez and a bus ticket to Garberville (for work). Last year Amtrak fucked me up because the train was late and they did not hold the bus, and I had all of my belongings then stolen in the process of waiting for the later bus. They assured me that this time that would not happen, that the bus *should* wait for the train, but I am going to try to make it to Martinez tonight anyway, if I can.

1922- It's the World Series again and for the second year straight I am watching it in some California brewery, this time at River City Brewing in downtown Sacramento (not an incredibly unique name by any means, as Sacramento is no more a river city than everyplace else). The St. Louis Cardinals, who just wouldn't die at home yesterday (twice coming back from two-run deficits at the last possible moment to take the game into extra innings, and eventually winning), make an incredibly boring to watch sport actually exciting, and are surprisingly up against the Rangers and now looking to win the World Series, tonight, in Game 7. I recommend the Woodenhead Amber.

Sacramento, CA

Martinez, CA- Martinez is one of the most unwelcoming towns I have ever been to, yet I opted to come here last night so that I do not again miss the 1030 bus north and have to wait around all day long for another, but also because I did not want to camp around the Amtrak station in Sacramento (I couldn't catch a freight train from Sacramento like I wanted so I took a brief, 40-minute ride aboard CalTrain, which is way more suited for the modern times and equipped with digital scanners and electronically printed seat-checks that are impossible to scam). Directly across from the Amtrak station in Martinez are an old black steam engine, a wooden ATSF boxcar, and an old ATSF caboose, all on display behind a low, wooden fence that is further distanced by a deep ditch (look out!). I slept there,

Martinez, CA

on the backside of the wooden boxcar, up on a wooden deck that was built as a display-entrance to the boxcar's door. It was a good thing I slept up there too because the Martinez raccoons were bad! All night long I could here them crawling around on dry leaves below, and one even came up the steps to the deck where I was asleep and nibbled at my foot through my sleeping bag!

Lots of trains came through blaring horns loudly throughout the night (a couple hotshots and lines of coil-cars, hoppers, and tankers that were always going too fast to catch on the fly). This morning, just before the sun rose, a cold chill filled the air making it too cold to fall back asleep.

November, 2011

Crescent City, CA- I hate hitchhiking. The forlornness and despair of it can really drive me crazy, and though I always end up getting a ride, anything that is 99% rejection is not an easy thing to do. It's sunny at least, and not raining as it closes in on around 2 P.M. I'm on the outskirts of Crescent City in California, standing on the 101 under a bright blue and white cirrus sky. From what I've seen just walking to this point, there is a significant CHP presence in Crescent City, so I hope someone picks me up soon. But also, because with Daylight Savings it gets dark early—around 4:30 or 5—so I don't have a lot of time to make it to the next town and I don't want to end up hitchhiking at night or sleeping on the road here. All these car that pass by are people riding alone with empty shotgun-seats. But what's the benefit of picking up a hitchhiker anyway? There's no transaction, no cash involved, and relationships almost never, ever stem from or are forged in hitchhiked rides. If anything, I feel like it's a lopsided gig: I get to go somewhere for free and it's a great story for me, while the person driving pays for everything and just gets a little companionship for what it's worth. And maybe that's a lot to them, but it's always seemed like it's worth much more to get a ride somewhere and not have to spend the money to get there than to satisfy your good-deed for the day (though I always do pick people up when I have the opportunity to drive). I am standing just past the Washington Blvd exit, right in front of the Begin Free-way sign, hoping I'm not in a place where the CHP is going to roll up and stop and

$7.95 U.S. / $9.99 CANADA

ISBN 978-1-62106-842-6

US$7.95

9 781621 068426 50795>

SKILLS TO CHANGE YOUR LIFE AND THE WORLD

www.Microcosm.Pub

2752 N WILLIAMS AVE • PORTLAND, OR 97227